THE WALL STREET JOURNAL.

COMPLETE
SMALL
BUSINESS
GUIDEBOOK

THE WALL STREET JOURNAL.

COMPLETE SMALL BUSINESS GUIDEBOOK

COLLEEN DEBAISE

THREE RIVERS PRESS
NEW YORK

Library of Congress Cataloging-in-Publication Data

DeBaise, Colleen.
The Wall Street Journal complete small business guidebook/
Colleen DeBaise.—1st ed.
  p. cm.
Includes index.
1. Small business. 2. Small business—Finance. 3. Entrepreneurship.
I. Title.
HD62.7.D43 2009
658.02'2—dc22   2009014775

ISBN 978-0-307-40893-8

Printed in the United States of America

Design by Mauna Eichner and Lee Fukui

Illustrations: p. 14, William Reiser c/o theispot.com; p. 25, 47, Adam McCauley c/o theispot.com; p. 35, Peter Hoey c/o theispot.com; p. 74, Aaron Meshon c/o theispot.com; p. 94, Riccardo Stampatori c/o theispot.com; p. 108, Jose Ortega c/o theispot.com; p. 140, JD King c/o theispot.com; p. 172, Dave Cutler c/o theispot.com; p. 190, Tim Lee c/o theispot.com; p. 200, John S. Dykes c/o theispot.com; p. 208, Tony Persiani c/o theispot.com.

10 9 8 7 6 5 4 3 2 1

CONTENTS

INTRODUCTION

When I meet with entrepreneurs, I hear about their dreams. They tell me why they think their product or service is exciting or game-changing or utterly unlike anything else that's out there. And no matter what stage of the process they're in, there's one thing that's unfailingly the same: there's passion.

I met with several start-up entrepreneurs at a holiday event in December 2008 when the markets had just collapsed and dire days, it seemed, were upon us. But at this gathering hosted by the networking group Savor the Success, I talked to new business owners who had just left the doldrums of corporate America and who were eager, at last, to be striking out on their own. The excitement in their voices was undeniable and contagious. It is not something you hear when talking to people who merely punch a clock or who while away the hours doing something they don't think is important or meaningful or fulfilling.

In the spring of 2009, I had the good fortune to sit down with one of those entrepreneurs whose story is enviable: he had come up with a unique product, been able to market it to the masses and had achieved great success and fortune. That entrepreneur was Jim Koch, the founder of Boston Beer Company, the leading independent brewer in the United States, and the creator of its well-loved Sam Adams beer.

We sat in his brewery in Boston, a sprawling brick building in the multicultural neighborhood of Jamaica Plain. Like most entrepreneurs, he didn't wear a suit or tie; he wore khakis and a company denim shirt with the Sam Adams logo. It was easy to forget that he now presides over a publicly traded company that makes some $400 million in annual revenue. In the early 1980s, he was working as a high-paid management consultant when he decided to quit, carry on a family tradition of brewing beer, and start a company that could craft a beverage more flavorful than mass-produced beer. In the first five minutes of our conversation, Koch quietly told me how he loved that beer cut through every demographic: it appealed to and connected people of every gender and ethnicity, from every place and socio-economic status.

Then, before I could ask him about his secrets of success, he volunteered his recipe for Sam Adams Spring Ale, a seasonal brew offered each spring. And that's when I heard that familiar excitement in his voice. "We start with water, yeast, malt and hops, the basic ingredients of every beer," he said in the manner of a storyteller about to spin a tale. "Then we add spices." Orange zest and a touch of coriander. Then rose hips, plums and hibiscus. Lemon zest, vanilla and a little anise— "just to spark some interest." Next, a dash of grains of paradise, a West African spice which has an "orchid-like aroma." And to finish it all, tamarind, an exotic ingredient often used in Asian cooking. "Wow," I said appreciatively. I wasn't sure what I had expected, but I had thought we'd be talking about more dry business topics, such as organizational goals or corporate governance. Instead, Koch sounded a lot like a start-up entrepreneur. "As a brewer, I can do that," said Koch, still eagerly talking about his recipe. "And that's just one beer."

Entrepreneurs—whether they're just out of the gate or have years of experience—always seem to have this fire inside them. That's not to say that business owners tell me it's easy to run the show—or that it doesn't consume their time, drain their energy or test their mettle. I once memorably heard a stressed-out entrepreneur say "there's no greater prison" than opening your own shop. But I also hear about the rewards. Perhaps more than anything, those who start their own business know they've got freedom . . . to follow their passion, to call the shots, to hire whom they want, to work when they want and to take their business as far as they want.

But what puts a person like Jim Koch on the path to success? Some of the very same strategies that are outlined in the pages of this book. He cemented his vision for a beer company by talking to mentors, most notably his dad, a retired brewer. He augmented his personal savings by raising start-up capital from friends and family. He used that money wisely and sparingly. He thought outside the box, essentially renting out breweries to make his beer when he didn't yet have enough in profits to build his own facility. He concentrated on making a quality, full-flavored product that was better than huge competitors' lighter beer. He wore many hats. Most notably, he learned to embrace salesmanship, something he originally dreaded but eventually found so enjoyable—and informative—that he still goes on sales calls. And he did what made him happy, something he advises anyone currently not satisfied in their line of work to do. "Find a business that you'll be happy doing even if doesn't make your rich," he said. "And make sure your product is better—or cheaper—than what others have."

If you are ready to turn your passion into a successful business, you've come to a trusted source for guidance. In Part One, we'll focus on the commitment you'll need and how to find enough cash to start and grow your business. In Part Two, we'll get into the mechanics of running a business, from hiring employees to investing in technology to staging your exit. And in Part Three, I'll tell you ways to strike work/life balance in the "always open for business" lifestyle of entrepreneurs.

Ultimately, there's something about starting a company with your own hands and building it to great heights that evokes the essence of the American dream. It's often said that small businesses are the engines of the economy and that it will be entrepreneurs—maybe yourself included—who lead this country to new heights in terms of innovation, job creation and overall well-being. I hope this guide shows you the way.

PART ONE

STARTING AND FUNDING YOUR OWN BUSINESS

CHAPTER 1

So You Think You Want to Be a Small Business Owner?

You probably bought this book to figure out where to find the money to start your own business. And you hope to learn the secrets of success—how to market, how to hire the best employees and how to get your products in all the top stores.

We'll get to that, of course. But first, before you make that leap into small business ownership, it's critical to see if entrepreneurship is right for you. If you've worked for someone else—and chances are you have—you probably haven't experienced the demands on your personal life, wallet and skill set that running a business entails.

First, let's take a look at that lifestyle part. There's been a resounding theme in my countless interviews with entrepreneurs: the business, especially in its early years, is going to require near constant attention. So if you're thinking about becoming your own boss, you'll want to be prepared for the rapid transformation that your lifestyle will undergo. For starters, you'll immediately give up corporate luxuries such as sick days or paid vacation time. And work/life balance—a challenge for any busy professional or corporate workaholic—will be difficult to strike. In Part Three of this book, I'll outline a few of the biggest lifestyle challenges and tell you how business owners have come up with unusual or creative ways to deal with them. But first, you need to think long and hard about whether that's the life for you.

Second, you'll undoubtedly be investing much of your personal savings in this new venture. It's always been difficult— make that pretty much impossible—for newbie entrepreneurs to get their hands on traditional bank or Small Business Administration–guaranteed loans. That was the case even before the recent meltdown in the financial industry. In the upcoming chapters in Part One, I'll take a look at how most people find the funds to launch and grow their start-ups, especially in these tough times. But you need to be realistic and recognize that you could lose a sizable chunk of your personal savings if your venture doesn't take off. Don't invest more than you can afford to lose.

Last, when it comes to skills, your talents surely will be tested, from your ability to market to your finesse with managing employees, all of which we'll cover in Part Two. And if you haven't already, you'll need to beef up your ability to manage finances. That can truly give your business a competitive edge—and, especially in an economic downturn, mean the difference between survival and failure. I remember being struck by a comment from one entrepreneur, Guy Jacobson, who left a career in investment banking behind to pursue his artistic dreams, starting the independent film company Priority Films in New York. While he's grateful to be creative in his new line of work, he tells me, "I can't just wear black all the time and act like an artist." He uses his financial background to run a lean, successful operation that's won accolades for its highly acclaimed films. No matter whether your true skill is frosting cakes or selling tires, you'll need financial know-how, too.

TAKE THE ENTREPRENEURSHIP QUIZ

Starting a business is a lot like becoming a parent. Not only do you have to prepare for your start-up emotionally and financially, but you have to be committed to its constant needs until it's mature enough to hum along on its own. And even then (much like a child) it will always need you in some capacity, no matter how old it gets.

Here are five questions to ask before you start your own business:

1. **Am I passionate about my product or service?**

   Let's face it: the start-up phase is stressful. You will find yourself questioning whether you've made the right decision, especially when the hours are long and the initial profits (if any) are lean. In interviews with entrepreneurs, I've heard many times how an unshakeable faith in the business kept them ticking, especially when customers were sparse, resources were limited and critics were many. Bobbi Brown, founder of the multimillion-dollar cosmetic line that bears her name, attributes her success to a passion for Brown No. 4—her creamy, natural-looking lipstick that she believed was unlike anything on the market. Brown ignored naysayers and launched her makeup line in 1991; four years later, the company was bought by cosmetics giant Estée Lauder for an undisclosed sum.

   As the business owner, you're also chief salesperson for your company. Your enthusiasm for your product or service—whether it's hand-knit sweaters or top-notch tax preparation—is often the difference that hooks customers, lands deals and attracts investors. Passion for your product or service is essential in building something larger than yourself. It's unwise to start down the path of entrepreneurship unless you've got a zeal that will get you through rough patches and keep you interested long after the initial enthusiasm has faded.

2. **What is my tolerance for risk?**

Whether it's quitting your day job or signing a lease on a new space, nothing about starting a business is for the faint of heart. Just ask Ina Garten, who bought a specialty-foods store called The Barefoot Contessa in East Hampton, New York, in 1978 and has since branched out into cookbooks, television and a line of products. Garten tells aspiring entrepreneurs that you have to "be willing to jump off the cliff and figure out how to fly on the way down."

That's because the risks of starting a business are many. Even with enough passion to launch a thousand ventures, you could find any number of circumstances hastening your failure: a location that turns out to be less than ideal, a problem with city or state zoning boards or a kink in the supply chain that can't easily be ironed out. There's no guarantee of success, or even a steady paycheck.

If you're risk-averse, entrepreneurship probably isn't the right path for you. But if you are willing to take chances and find appeal in the benefits of ownership—being your own boss, setting your own schedule and directly profiting from all the hard work—then entrepreneurship might be a solid fit.

If you think your risk tolerance is fairly high, great. This book will help you to learn more about managing your risk through careful planning—such as writing a thorough business plan, getting advice from a mentor and talking to other business owners about the experiences they've had.

3. **Am I good at making decisions?**

No one else is going to make them for you when you own your own business. If you are not decisive or adapt-

MAKING TOUGH CALLS IN THE MIDST OF A STORM

Many business owners who kept their operations afloat after Hurricane Katrina devastated New Orleans in 2005 attributed their recovery to quick decision making.

Take Greg Mangiaracina, who was born and raised in the Big Easy. He founded A-Pro Home Inspection in 1994, and at the time of Katrina, it was thriving. He had begun franchising in 2004, and in September 2005, he was expecting a group of twelve new franchisees to come to his New Orleans training facility. Katrina changed all that. As the storm approached, he and his family evacuated to a hotel in Atlanta, where they watched on television as the surge broke the levees and swept into the city.

In that moment, Mangiaracina knew bringing new franchisees to New Orleans—at least anytime soon—would be impossible. Even as the hurricane continued to rage, he began talking out a relocation plan with his wife. They nixed Chicago, Memphis, Tampa and Phoenix, finally deciding on San Antonio, Texas, a city five hundred miles away from New Orleans with a decent-sized population, convenient location and good schools for their two young sons. Mangiaracina worked eighteen hours a day from the hotel to plan the relocation and to salvage his business. His quick decision making paid off. On September 28, 2005, almost a month to the day after the hurricane struck, he greeted the group of twelve franchisees at A-Pro's new headquarters in San Antonio, and by the time the first anniversary of Katrina rolled around, the company's revenues had doubled.

able to change, an entrepreneurial life probably isn't for you. Consider how you might handle these early decisions: Do I work from home or do I lease office space? Do I hire employees? Do I pursue high-end clients or sell to the masses? Do I incorporate? Do I advertise? Do I borrow money from friends or family? Do I use my entire savings?

This book will help you answer these and other questions, but if you're already feeling overwhelmed, keep in mind that the decision-making process only gets more complicated as time goes on. Once you have employees or clients depending on you, you'll face additional choices: Do I move into a larger space, even if it's farther away from staff members' homes? Do I shift the company's direction, and possibly lose valued customers, to make more profits? Do I offer health care benefits? Do I cut health insurance because of the cost?

In short, as the business owner, you are the ultimate decision maker. The choices you make can lead to success or downfall, so you must feel confident in your ability to make the right call.

4. **Am I willing to take on numerous responsibilities?**

While a corporate employee focuses on a special skill or role within the larger corporation, a business owner must contribute everything to the business. Solo entrepreneurs in particular must be versatile and play a number of roles, from chief salesperson and bookkeeper to head marketer and bill collector. This can lead to tough situations, such as needing to get paid but not wanting to alienate a good client. (For more tips on bill collecting, see Chapter 9.) Successful entrepreneurs must find ways to integrate and manage these many facets of small business ownership. If juggling many roles doesn't suit you, entrepreneurship probably won't, either.

The recent economic downturn has made it more important than ever for business owners to have a good working knowledge of their companies' finances. Many entrepreneurs tell me they were woefully unprepared to handle the books when they started out. While you will undoubtedly learn much on this topic from getting your hands dirty, the more knowledge you have in advance, the better prepared you'll be. For starters, it's critical to un-

PLACES TO FIND A SUPPORT NETWORK

Entrepreneurs' Organization

www.eonetwork.org

Founded more than twenty years ago, this membership group offers peer-to-peer learning and other ways for entrepreneurs to connect.

Women Presidents' Organization

www.womenpresidentsorg.com

The WPO is an opportunity for top women entrepreneurs (whose businesses must meet a certain revenue criterion) to meet and act as sounding boards for one another.

LifeWork Leadership

www.lifeworkleadership.org

This faith-based group offers leadership training though monthly classes and retreats.

derstand how cash flows in and out of your company. (For more on how one business owner learned to handle finances, see page 82.)

Because of their numerous roles, even the best small business owners can often feel overwhelmed, overloaded and frustrated. Entrepreneurs I've interviewed say it's easy to spend too much time getting too little done, leading to disappointment and burnout. But there are some things you can do to improve your multitasking skills and ease some of the stress of running the show, which you'll learn about in this book.

And that leads us to our last question.

5. **Will I be able to avoid burnout?**

Working seven days a week, losing touch with friends, abandoning old hobbies and interests and not making time for loved ones can quickly lead to burnout in the midst of starting up—and ultimately to business failure.

That's what happened to James Zimbardi, an entrepreneur in Orlando, Florida, who says he didn't know any better when he started his first company in 1997 and worked as hard as possible, for as long as possible, until his creativity, enthusiasm and energy were sapped. By 2002, he was a broken man—the business took a downturn, and so did his personal life. Now Zimbardi is at work on his second company, Allgen Financial Services, and sticking to better habits, such as not working on Sundays, making time for hobbies such as sailing and salsa dancing, and building close ties with other business owners through a faith-based support network.

Still, it's tough to step away. Most entrepreneurs have strong work ethics and practically eat and breathe their businesses because they are so passionate about them. Zimbardi says, "I'm wired to go in that direction, so I have to put things in place to keep me honest."

Take some time to mull over these questions, do some soul-searching, and then if you think you have what it takes, go for it. Once you've taken the plunge, you'll find yourself figuring the rest out on the way down, with the information in the rest of this book acting as your parachute.

CHAPTER 2

WRITING A BUSINESS PLAN

N ow that you understand the commitment, let's walk through the basics of launching and growing a company, starting with getting it all on paper. In other words, it's time to begin crafting your business plan.

Your written plan describes your business, outlines your goals and serves as a road map for future activities—everything from handling unforeseen complications to repaying borrowed money. It's a document that should grow with your business, undergoing constant tweaks as your big idea evolves from a concept into a successful company.

A strong business plan is essentially the cornerstone of your business, and yet many entrepreneurs drag their feet when it comes to writing one—possibly because it involves a good deal of work and may bring back childhood memories of writing a tedious book report on summer vacation. But it's critical that you not only organize your thoughts on how you intend to run your business but also formalize your plan in writing. Here's why:

- **It forces you to identify your (and your company's) strengths and weaknesses.** You don't want to start a company that is flawed before it's even in business. Sitting down, writing a plan, thinking about everything you bring to the table (whether that's a passion for cupcakes or an enthusiasm for medical software) and considering everything you're lacking (whether that's salesmanship or computer skills) can give you a realistic snapshot of your odds of success. Your goal should be to focus on your strengths and fix any problems that could hamper your growth.

INFORMAL VS. FORMAL

Typically, an entrepreneur who's seeking investors, lenders or partners will need to devote the most time and energy to writing a formal business plan. If you're not seeking any of those, or need to jump into the market quickly to sell your product or service, then you can create a more informal plan that will undoubtedly help you plan, guide your decisions and keep you on track. What's the minimum that any business plan—including an informal one—should include? A company description and mission statement, plus an overview of your target market, competition, sales strategy and marketing plan. And don't forget a cash flow statement.

• **It helps you figure out how much money you'll need.** Entrepreneurs chronically underestimate how much money they'll need to start a business. (For more on figuring out start-up expenses, see Chapter 3.) Keep in mind: a lack of capital is one of the top reasons why businesses struggle or close during the first year. Writing a plan forces you to get a handle on where your money will come from, where it will go and whether it will be enough—not only to get your business off the ground, but also to sustain growth in subsequent years.

• **It gives you clear direction, which can help eliminate stress.** As a business owner, you often have to juggle multiple roles—everything from bookkeeper to CEO—and that can leave you feeling distracted, disorganized and overwhelmed. A document that outlines your mission and plans for the future can prevent overload, help you set realistic goals, keep you on track and boost your productivity.

- **It will serve as a resume when you seek lenders, investors or partners.** Most lenders, and certainly any professional investor such as an angel or venture capitalist, will expect to see a business plan before giving you money. Even if you're not seeking outside money, a business plan can be helpful when renting space (a landlord might demand to see one) or seeking a business partner. For partners who start a business together, writing a plan ensures that everyone is on the same page when it comes to the company's mission and strategies.

- **It makes you evaluate the market for your product or service and size up the competition.** As you write your plan you'll research the current market and see how your product or service might fare against existing offerings. By analyzing your competition, you'll get a sense of how to price your product or service, how to target the right customers and how to make your company stand out, particularly in a crowded marketplace.

As you assemble your business plan, you'll see opportunities to fine-tune your concept, avoid problems that could become disasters and ultimately increase your odds of success. We'll look more closely at each component of a strong business plan, so you'll understand how this document plays such an integral role in the future of your company.

YOUR BUSINESS PLAN COMPONENTS

There's really no set way to write a business plan, although most follow a similar formula. Ideally, a business plan should be clear and succinct—perhaps twenty to twenty-five pages in length—and contain the following elements: an executive summary, a detailed company description, a market analysis and a financial plan. Check out the sample business plan for Jolly's Java, a start-up bakery and coffee shop, in Appendix 1 on page 209.

BUSINESS PLAN CONTESTS

A business plan competition at a college or university is an excellent way for an entrepreneur to develop a fledgling idea, get professional feedback and—in some cases—attract publicity. Winners often receive cash prizes ranging from $10,000 to $125,000 per contest, plus accounting or marketing help.

Business plan competitions are generally for MBA candidates, but in recent years many schools have changed the rules to allow alumni and non-students to compete (generally, if you are not enrolled at the school, you must team up with a student who is). Business plan contests are primarily held in the spring. Participants usually prepare the business plan under faculty supervision and ultimately present it to a panel of judges. Here are a few of the more well-known competitions:

Moot Corp—University of Texas at Austin
www.mootcorp.org
Dubbing itself the "Super Bowl" of business plan competitions, Moot Corp offers a prize package worth $100,000 in cash, business consulting services and mentoring. Plus, the winning team gets to ring the opening bell of the Nasdaq Stock Market.

Stern Business Plan Competition—New York University
http://w4.stern.nyu.edu/berkley/bpc.cfm?doc_id=6306
NYU's contest awards $75,000 to winning teams, plus another $100,000 to winning social entrepreneurs (those who use business skills to tackle world problems).

Rice Business Plan Competition—Rice University
www.alliance.rice.edu/alliance/RBPC.asp
The Rice contest offers $125,000 for the grand prize winner, plus participants can network with experienced venture capitalists, early-stage investors and successful entrepreneurs who serve as judges.

Here's a rundown of each component:

EXECUTIVE SUMMARY

The most important part of any business plan, the executive summary, serves as a compact version of your great idea. Keep it brief (even a few paragraphs is fine), use straightforward language and don't forget to communicate your passion for your idea. (See page 213 for Jolly's Java's Executive Summary.)

The executive summary is essentially your sales pitch, which you will present or deliver to wow investors, lenders, vendors, suppliers, potential employees, partners and, of course, customers or clients. Explain what your company does, who your customers are, why you and your management team are expressly qualified to run the business, how you plan to market your products and services and what your financial projections are. Make sure to include a brief mission statement that encompasses your business philosophy and positioning. You may want to write the executive summary last, taking pieces from some of your other sections, but it should be the first thing readers see. Keep the wording positive; your aim is to make your business shine on the page.

DETAILED COMPANY DESCRIPTION

Here you'll what to include some of the logistical and other nitty-gritty details, such as your company's physical location, facilities and equipment; its domain name; the specific products or services offered; and details of staffing needs and ongoing projects (include dates for completion). You'll also want to describe the company's management team and outline the company's legal structure, such as a regular C corporation or a limited liability company. (See Chapter 11 for more details on which legal structures is right for your business.) Include information about your industry, such as trends and major players.

RESOURCES FOR WRITING A BUSINESS PLAN

Small Business Administration's Write a Business Plan
http://www.sba.gov/smallbusinessplanner/plan/writeabusinessplan/
index.html
The SBA's website contains a tutorial and FAQs about business plans.

Bplans.com
www.bplans.com
This site offers articles, free sample business plans, and software for
writing business plans.

NFIB's Small Business Toolbox
http://www.nfib.com; search "business plan."
The National Federation of Independent Business provides resources and
tips for writing business plans.

Market Analysis and Plan

Describe who your customers are, and take a look at any other
companies that are currently meeting their needs. Include
geographic location, age and gender of potential customers.
If you're a business-to-business company, focus on the size and
industry of your target clients. Try to estimate how many customers you'll have and how you'll reach them. Include details
of your pricing plan, sales strategy and promotional or advertising activities—including, if appropriate, how you'll blend a
brick-and-mortar operation with online activities. Be realistic
about your competitors, and discuss how you will overcome
any barriers to the marketplace.

Financial Plan

Include a projected profit-and-loss statement (see page 222 for Jolly's Java's projected P&L), which is a forecast of how much you expect to sell and how much you anticipate to earn after deducting expenses. Make sure the numbers are realistic, something many overly optimistic entrepreneurs fail to do. Include a cash flow table, which will demonstrate your ability to pay bills and keep yourself afloat. (See Chapter 9 for more on financial statements.) Seek the assistance of an accountant or bookkeeper, especially if you are still learning about business finances. You'll also want to include a description of your funding requirements if you are seeking a loan or equity financing. Include a section of major risks you'll face and how you will respond to each.

CHAPTER 3

THE
LEAN YEARS

In addition to a surefire idea, there's one thing every business needs to get started: money.

Finding the funding for a small business is a lot like scraping together enough cash for your first home. To come up with a down payment for a home mortgage, you might tap into personal savings and turn to loved ones for contributions. And then you might use credit cards to cover moving expenses, new furniture and other costs associated with home ownership.

But one stark difference between launching a business and buying a home is this: there's really no equivalent of a mortgage for newbie entrepreneurs. That's because lenders such as traditional banks simply don't find start-up ventures with minimal cash flow and unproven track records to be attractive clients. If the business goes belly-up—and SBA statistics show that about one-third of new businesses don't make it past the two-year mark—then the lender has little chance of getting its money back. In contrast, if a home owner defaults on a mortgage, at least the lender can seize the home, sell it off and get a good chunk of that money back.

That means most small business owners have to cobble together money for their start-up through a piecemeal combination of savings, credit cards and cash from "informal investors," such as parents, family friends or even neighbors. As revenues grow and the owner becomes wiser and more experienced, then it might be possible to successfully secure conventional loans or cash infusions from professional investors.

As you think about possible sources of funding, you also have to ask yourself: How much cash do I need, exactly? The answer, of course, varies greatly with the type of business you plan to launch. A small manufacturer, for instance, probably requires a hefty budget to cover the cost of leasing a warehouse, buying industrial equipment and training staff. A solo home-based entrepreneur, on the other hand, might only need a shoestring budget to buy a desk, order a high-speed Internet connection and get a professional-looking website designed.

In one SBA study, eight hundred individuals in the process of starting a business were asked to project start-up costs. Their estimates were surprisingly modest: solo entrepreneurs predicted they'd need an average of $6,000, while team-based entrepreneurs (that is, companies with two or more cofounders) figured on $20,000.

Whether those modest estimates are realistic is another story. Another study, by Babson College, found that the average amount needed to start a business is $65,000. Most research suggests that entrepreneurs frequently underestimate start-up costs and overestimate initial revenues, leading to major cash flow problems.

Because the most important resource in starting your business and financing its ongoing operations is cash, it's vitally important to figure out exactly how much you'll need—long before opening your doors. This chapter will help you accurately estimate your start-up costs and initial revenues to increase your chances of surviving your first year of business and beyond.

CALCULATING START-UP COSTS

Got a pen handy? To best estimate your start-up costs, you'll need to make a list—and the more detailed the better. A smart way to start is to brainstorm everything you'll need, from tangible goods (such as inventory, equipment and fixtures) to professional services (such as remodeling, advertising and legal work). Then, start calculating how much you'll need to pay for all those goods and services.

Some of the expenses incurred during the start-up phase will be one-time costs, such as the fee for printing up your brochures, creating your LLC or acquiring a permit, while others will be ongoing, such as rent, insurance or employees' salaries. In general, it's best to use a two-step process. First, come up with an estimate of one-time costs needed to get your doors open, and then develop an operating budget for the first six months or even the first year of the business. Check out the sample worksheet provided by the Better Business Bureau in Appendix 2 on page 242.

The categories listed below will aid you in completing your list of costs for opening and operating a small business:

> **OOPS, WE FORGOT ABOUT THAT**
>
> Why do small business owners underestimate how much they'll need? Inexperience plays a large role. Natalka Burian and Betsy Nadel, who started Hanger Bar and Boutique in Manhattan's East Village in 2004 at the youthful ages of twenty-two and twenty-three, say they simply forgot to factor in ongoing or "carrying" costs—money needed to maintain inventory, rent, utilities, taxes and other expenses. Keep in mind that you might not have sales right away, so you'll need a reserve to keep the business afloat in the initial start-up phase.

Location.
Think about how much you'll need to pay for rent, to make improvements to the space or for full-scale renovations.

DO I NEED TO PROVIDE BENEFITS TO EMPLOYEES?

You are not required to provide health benefits to employees unless you are an employer in Hawaii or Massachusetts. (Hawaii requires companies to provide health coverage to all full-time employees; Massachusetts businesses with more than ten employees are required to offer pretax health plans to employees.) To be sure, the U.S. health care system is in a state of flux, and lawmakers may ultimately require more employers in all states to provide some level of coverage for workers.

Generally, you do not have to provide a retirement plan for your employees, although there are special rules about including employees if you start a certain plan for yourself. For more on that, see Chapter 15.

While you may not be required to provide benefits, you may wish to offer coverage, if you can afford it, as a way to recruit or retain your workforce.

Inventory.
Figure out the cost of raw materials, plus any production costs, or the wholesale prices of products you'll be selling. Calculate shipping and packaging costs, sales commissions and other costs related to the sale of your product.

Equipment.
Add up how much it costs to buy or lease computers, copiers, telephones, heavy-duty machinery or other fixtures.

Employees.
Calculate salaries and wages, plus benefits you would offer, and don't forget payroll-related taxes, overtime pay and workers' compensation.

Marketing.
Figure out how much you'll pay for new stationery, marketing materials, advertising campaigns, the sign above your door and meals or entertainment with clients.

Administrative and operational costs.
Keep track of how much you'll need to pay for insurance (to protect against property damage, business interruption and floods) and office supplies. Don't forget utilities, a commonly overlooked expense, and other charges, such as phone and Internet service, cleaning and property maintenance.

Professional fees and permits.
Add up how much you'll pay for your attorney, accountant or other advisor or consultant. Factor in what you'll need to pay for permits or licenses related to your business.

If you're still having trouble figuring out how much money you need, do research on other companies in your industry and region of the country. Talk to other business owners about how they figured out start-up costs—and ask specifically about expenses they forgot. The SBA offers free counseling through its Small Business Development Centers and its affiliate, SCORE. You can also seek advice from an accountant or attorney accustomed to dealing with small businesses.

When in doubt about your projections, you should always err on the side of overestimating your up-front investment cost and underestimating sales. Eric van Merkensteijn, a University of Pennsylvania business professor who left academia in the late 1990s to open a restaurant in Philadelphia, offers this advice: Figure out your start-up costs, then double that number. Then double it again. Only then will you have a realistic number, says the professor, who closed the business in 2004 and returned to campus.

SOURCES OF FUNDS TO GET YOUR BUSINESS STARTED

Now that you've calculated how much you need, next comes the tricky part: getting your hands on the cash.

Here are the top sources of funding for most small-business owners:

TRIMMING THE BUDGET

What if you don't have enough money to start? In the likely event that happens, start crossing off expendable items—such as pricey renovations, full-color ads or even staff members—from your list. And get creative.

Maribel Araujo, a Venezuelan native who opened a small eatery in New York City in 2003, did all the handiwork (along with husband Gato) when she found a vacant storefront suitable for her restaurant. The couple poured $60,000 into the business, mostly using their own savings and money from friends and family. But by cleaning, painting and renovating the flooring themselves, while an artistic friend painted a large mural on the wall and another friend made the counter, Araujo estimates they saved about $40,000.

ADDITIONAL RESOURCES

SCORE: Can You Afford to Start a Business?
www.tsbc.com/sbo/score/module.aspx?mid=103&cid=1

BPlans.com Starting Costs Estimator
www.bplans.com/common/calculators/startingcosts.cfm

Better Business Bureau Tips on Small Business Start-up Costs
www.bbb.org/ALERTS/article.asp?ID=605

1. PERSONAL SAVINGS

It doesn't matter if the economy is soaring or the nation is still digging itself out of a recession: your first financial resource for starting a business will always be your personal stash. That said, with more Americans carrying around credit card debt than ever before and many failing to save enough for retirement, your personal savings may not offer much in the way of seed capital for a new business. (Don't have any savings? I don't advise starting a business.)

CAN I WRITE OFF START-UP COSTS?

Here's good news for the newbie business owner: you're entitled to deduct up to $5,000 of start-up costs in the year in which you open your business. (That number is reduced when start-up costs rise above $50,000, and disappears when costs go over $55,000.) Any remainder would be amortized over a fifteen-year period. So if you shell out $8,000 to start a business, you can deduct $5,000 of those expenses. The balance, or $3,000, would be amortized over fifteen years.

The write-off is known as the Section 195 deduction after a provision in the tax code. If your start-up costs are high and you don't qualify for the deduction, you can still amortize costs over fifteen years. For more information visit www.irs.gov.

Exactly how much you should dig into your own pocket can depend on your life stage. A thirty-year-old single person who's built up a sizable savings is in a different situation than a forty-year-old parent who's the sole breadwinner for a family. For that reason, the percentage of savings that you pour into a new, untested business is very much an individual or family decision. A married person who wants to start a business also has to have a serious discussion with a spouse about how much of the couple's joint savings account should be used to launch a start-up.

There are, however, a few rules of thumb. One is to not use *all* of your savings. Keep a good chunk of money in your savings or money market account not only for personal needs but also as a reserve for unplanned expenses that might arise in the first year of your business. In general, a good personal finance strategy is to keep an emergency fund—usually about three months' worth of the fixed costs in your life, such as rent, car payments, property taxes or insurance premiums—in the event you lose a steady paycheck. For a newbie entrepreneur, you may need to have considerably more than three months' worth of personal expenses saved up, especially since initial sales may not come in as quickly as you anticipate.

Another rule of thumb: don't be tempted by retirement savings. Of all the ways to bootstrap a business, dipping into a 401(k), IRA or other tax-favored retirement vehicle is the choice of last resort. Most financial advisors say don't do it at all. Not only are you subject to early withdrawal penalties and income taxes, but you'll lose that tax-deferred compounding that could have built up a sizable nest egg.

To see what all this might mean for you, consider Agnes, a twenty-nine-year-old aspiring entrepreneur, who wants to quit her sales job at a big pharmaceutical company to start her own matchmaking service for serious romantics. She's done her homework and has calculated she needs about $30,000 to launch her new venture (the money would go toward renting a small office, paying for an advertising campaign, and having a professional website designed). She's got $10,000 in a money market fund, $50,000 in a 401(k), a low-interest personal credit card and a great relationship with Mom and Dad.

She's thinking about taking $5,000 from the money market account but leaving the remaining $5,000 to keep herself afloat for several months. Then she's considering dipping into that 401(k) for about $10,000, which represents 20 percent of her total retirement savings. She's heard most plans let you borrow 50 percent of the plan's worth.

Next, she plans to talk to Mom and Dad for a $10,000 contribution to her dream. That gets her up to $25,000. For the last $5,000, she's planning to use her credit card in a judicious manner, such as for managing expenses as the business begins operations.

Does her plan make financial sense?

I asked Stacy Francis, a certified financial planner in New York City, to give us her thoughts. Nope, Agnes's current plan needs some help, says Francis. The financial planner suggests five steps:

1. Agnes should get a part-time job to help her save up an extra $5,000 to start the business. After she quits the sales job, that part-time job can continue to help supplement her income.

2. She should ask Mom and Dad for more. See if they can contribute $25,000. (For more on borrowing from friends and family, see below.)

3. Agnes should leave her personal savings of $10,000 alone. She should have a robust emergency fund, as salaries are lean (or nonexistent) in the early years of running any new business.

4. Under no circumstances should Agnes touch her 401(k) or any other retirement plan. (Additional note: many corporations set firm rules about borrowing from a 401(k). Generally, you can borrow for hardship or home purchases, but not to start your own business. Also, you typically have to pay back the loan immediately upon leaving the company.)

5. Never use personal credit cards to fund business costs. The low interest rate can easily jump, plus you are taking on personal liability for the business. (For more on credit cards, see next section.)

2. FAMILY AND FRIENDS

There's a reason why cash from family and friends is often called "love money": usually no one else will fund a newbie entrepreneur's dreams. Babson College, which has studied startups, found that two-thirds of the average $65,000 needed to launch a business comes from the entrepreneur's savings, while the balance comes from informal investors—most typically, family members and friends.

HOWDY, PARTNER

If you're short on cash, you might consider finding yourself a business partner who can offer financial resources, share the risk and bring complementary abilities to the table. But finding an entrepreneurial soul mate can be tricky. A business partnership is a lot like a marriage—it's a trusting, intimate relationship, and nothing short of your livelihood is at stake if the partnership fails. That's why many people turn to family members—frequently siblings or spouses—or even childhood friends for help in running a business.

Denise Brewer and Monica Griffin, co-owners of American Document Imaging in Tulsa, Oklahoma, met when their children attended school together. Brewer, who worked in TV, and Griffin, who worked in oil and gas, became running buddies, and used to chat while jogging about a shared dream to run a successful business while taking care of the kids. In 2004, the two pooled resources and talents and opened up a document-imaging center, with a special room where their kids can play or do work after school. What makes their partnership so successful, they say, are their complementary skills—Brewer brings communications and marketing abilities to ADI, while Griffin, whose specialty had been buying oil-producing wells and making them run more efficiently, brings her business skills. The two also say they spent months researching their idea and polishing their business plan before they launched—and advise other entrepreneurs to get to know their partner before diving in.

Can't find your dream business partner so easily? Write up a description of the person you're looking for, and e-mail it to your contacts or post on alumni listservs. Attend networking events at business schools (which are often open to business professionals as well as alums) and check with counselors at SBA Small Business Development Centers or SCORE.

Once you've found a partner, don't forget to draw up a partnership agreement, which (much like a prenuptial agreement) spells out how much cash or property each brings to the relationship, and outlines what happens if either one of you wants out.

It can be tricky, however, taking money from friends or family members. Do you give them equity in the company? Do you structure the transaction as a formal loan? If so, how soon do you start repaying them? And what happens if you can't pay them back?

The best thing to do, says Babson professor William Bygrave, is to make sure the people putting up the money are fully aware that they might lose it all. (That's why it's not appropriate for an older relative, for instance, to invest his or her nest egg in your business.) In his research, Bygrave found that most informal investors shell out the cash out of altruism— and most don't expect to be repaid. In fact, he doesn't advise that start-up entrepreneurs formalize the terms of the loan, as that gives the impression that the money will soon be repaid. Instead, he suggests that the deal stay loosely structured until the business has enough cash flow to afford regular payments, which might be several years down the road.

Of course, there are varying opinions on whether this is the best approach. The IRS, or even a jealous sibling, might question whether the cash that Mom and Dad contributed to your business is a loan, a gift or a contribution of capital. Lenders, such as a traditional bank, might want to know if that lump of cash on the balance sheet is a gift or a loan. And the relationship between the informal investor and the entrepreneur might become strained if there aren't clear expectations about whether that money will be repaid.

To avoid these gray areas, some business owners may want to consider using a service that provides documentation for peer-to-peer lending. For instance, Virgin Money in Waltham, Massachusetts, structures arrangements between business owners and their relatives or friends, setting up customized loans with flexible terms, lengthy grace periods and rates or payment schedules favorable to the business owner. One of the best parts about the service, president Asheesh Advani says, is that it forces the parties involved to have a conversation about what their expectations are.

What are the advantages of structuring the money as a formal loan? For starters, the business owner can deduct interest payments, just like a regular loan. And if the business goes belly-up, the lender can claim a capital loss. In the event the business doesn't succeed, the friend or family member becomes a creditor with more of a chance of recouping the loan during a bankruptcy proceeding.

But there are advantages to the money being simply a gift, too. Obviously, the entrepreneur won't have to deal with the pressure of paying anyone back. And he or she will have an easier time getting a bank loan down the road if that cash is a gift (as opposed to debt). For the friend and family member, there are advantages, too, especially from an estate-planning perspective. For the more affluent, it's best to give the money as part of the annual gift amount that doesn't trigger the gift tax. (In 2009, an individual could give $13,000; a couple could give $26,000). Ultimately, it depends on how your informal investors feel most comfortable providing you the money, but given the choice, I'd recommend accepting the money as a gift.

When do you give a friend or family member equity or an ownership stake in your business? Rarely, unless you truly believe your start-up is a high-growth company that eventually will go public or be bought out. For wealthier friends or family members, structuring the cash as equity also can cause an estate-planning headache, especially if the business takes off and adds tremendous value to their estates.

3. CREDIT CARDS

It's tempting to use plastic to fund your start-up. And many entrepreneurs do, particularly when other options are so limited. Research from the SBA found that the number of small businesses carrying debt rose 25 percent in 2005 as a result of credit cards.

But it's important to understand the risks before racking up too much credit card debt. A good word to keep in mind is

THE FAMILY PLAN

In 2005, Ken Wisnefski Jr. needed a cash infusion for his two-year-old online vendor business but had few places left to turn. He had already exhausted his savings, stretched out credit lines and dug into home equity. Traditional banks didn't think he had enough of a track record for a loan, and professional investors (angels and venture capitalists) either demanded too much control or wanted to see more revenues.

Fortunately, Wisnefski had one last source to tap: Dad. With a handshake, he secured $100,000 in financing at 0 percent interest to grow his business, VendorSeek.com, to the next level. Best of all, the "loan" was payable whenever he could pay it back.

The cash did come with an interesting twist, though: Wisnefski's father, Ken senior, a former entrepreneur himself, wanted a position with the company. The elder Wisnefski was approaching retirement age but wasn't ready—financially or otherwise—for his golden years. Plus he thought his years of sales experience could help his son. So now he spends his days as VendorSeek's senior account manager, for which he receives a salary and benefits. While the two men sometimes butt heads, the arrangement has worked out well—and VendorSeek's annual revenues by 2007 had quadrupled to about $4 million. Profits have been reinvested, and the younger Wisnefski has paid back about $25,000 to his father so far, making the payments when he can. "It's worked out to be a good fit for both of us," he says.

easy—it's easy to get the money, but it's also easy to get in over your head. In the rush to start, and driven by a desire to make the business succeed at all costs, too many entrepreneurs start using credit cards too freely, and without reading the fine print. They don't know the annual percentage rate. They fail to guard against rising fees. They don't understand the fees for late payments. Before long, they're swimming in debt—and under that much more pressure to get more clients, make more sales or complete more projects to stay afloat.

Then again, some business owners use credit wisely. What's the best way to do that? Start by using credit cards for a limited number of expenses that can be paid back quickly. Understand your company's cash flow—that is, the money coming in from sales versus money going out for rent, inventory and any other expenses. Make sure you can handle the debt without ever being late, which almost always triggers a higher interest rate.

It's also wise to apply for a business credit card. In the early years, a business credit card will require a personal guarantee—meaning you and your credit score are on the line if you have trouble paying bills. So why use one? A business credit card is a great way to keep work-related expenses separate from personal expenses, which will come in handy during tax season when you want to track deductions (including the business card's finance charges and annual fees). Charging and paying off business-related items also is a good way to establish a credit track record, which can help down the road when you search for bank loans or venture capital.

SHOULD I PICK A BUSINESS CARD BASED ON ITS REWARDS PROGRAMS?

Whether it's cash-back for office supplies or discounts on hotel stays, business cards often woo entrepreneurs with fancy perks and reward programs. But should you pick a card based on its rewards program? Not if the rewards cost you more than they're worth. If you're quick at paying off debts, take a look, but don't let the rewards distract you. If you plan to carry a balance, it's wiser to choose a card with the lowest APR (and pay attention to whether that rate changes after an introductory period).

4. HOME EQUITY LOANS OR LINES OF CREDIT

Are you sitting on equity? If you're a homeowner, the seed money for your small business might be no further than the four walls in front of you.

About 30 percent of small business owners tap into home equity to help finance their business, according to an August 2007 survey

ADDITIONAL RESOURCES

BusinessCreditSuccess.com
Founded by Gerri Detweiler and Garrett Sutton, this site supplies information for future and current business owners on leveraging business credit.

CardRatings.com
A comprehensive free site for comparing credit card offers.

CardWeb.com
This site maintains lists of the best business credit cards.

by Discover Small Business Watch. In general, a home-based loan can be a smart, inexpensive way to access funds, especially if those funds go toward consolidating credit card debt or up-dating an old kitchen or bath to increase your home's resale value. But whether home equity is a wise strategy for funding your business depends on a number of factors. The most pressing thing to keep in mind is that if the business doesn't succeed and you default on the loan, you could lose your home.

If you're considering going the home equity route, you'll probably either take out a home equity loan, sometimes called a second mortgage, or set up a home equity line of credit, or HELOC. A home equity loan, much like your original mortgage, is a lump sum that you pay off over time, usually at a fixed rate through scheduled monthly payments. A HELOC functions more like a credit card, allowing you to borrow chunks of money at a time and pay off the outstanding balance, usually at a rate that varies over time.

The best time to tap into home equity is during a strong economy, when rates are stable and home properties are rising in value. In recent years, as the housing market has collapsed in many areas of the countries, securing a home equity loan has become far more difficult. You'll need to make sure your credit history is strong, and you'll likely have to show that you or your spouse has a dependable source of income to repay the loan. Values of homes have dropped, meaning you may have far less equity than just a few years ago. In general, you should have at least 20 percent equity in your home before searching for a home equity loan; otherwise you'll need to buy private mortgage insurance. Monthly premiums for PMI have risen sharply in areas where housing prices have plummeted.

Budgeting is key to figuring out whether a home-based loan is right for you. Keep in mind that while you may see advertised low rates, you'll probably get those good deals only if you have a high credit score (above 700) and are borrowing less than 80 percent of your home's value. Shop around to see what kind of rate and term you can get, and don't forget to factor in closing costs. Determine how much you can afford to pay back each month (remember, a late payment can wreak havoc on your credit score and lead to higher rates). Because of the concerns, some business owners use a home equity loan for only a portion of start-up costs, relying on other sources (personal savings or informal investors) to finance the rest.

Of course, home-based loans offer many advantages, typically including lower rates than traditional loans or credit cards. In most cases, the interest is tax deductible on a loan up to $100,000, although consult with your accountant or tax advisor for details on your particular situation.

5. GRANTS AND CONTESTS

It's not easy to find free money for your business. But for a particularly creative or diligent entrepreneur, it's possible.

Some state and local governments offer incentives to encourage business development in underserved areas or struggling industries. In Miami-Dade County, the Mom and Pop Small Business Grant Program provides financial and technical assistance to qualified small businesses. Alaska has offered

BORROWING MONEY FROM STRANGERS

 A growing number of online lending networks—Prosper.com, LendingClub.com and others—allow entrepreneurs to secure small loans (usually less than $25,000) from strangers. Business owners who go this route say they're able to get money more quickly and with less paperwork than with a traditional bank. Typically, here's how it works: an entrepreneur creates an online listing, explaining how much money he or she wants, what it will be used for and how much he or she wants to pay as an interest rate. Lenders can peruse the listings (which usually include information about a borrower's credit history) and decide which applications to fund. Some lenders say they're drawn to online networks as a way to earn better returns than investments in stocks or bonds, and because they like helping out real people.

$25,000 in grants to salmon harvesters through a revitalization program for the state's fisheries. Check your state's economic development agency's website for a listing of programs you might be eligible for.

A number of business groups offer modest sums of grant money to small employers. The National Association for the Self-Employed, for instance, offers small grants (usually up to $5,000) for business owners with fewer than ten employees to buy equipment, pay for advertising or fund some other specific business need. For more on NASE grants, visit www.nase.org/grants.

Numerous credit card companies and corporations that cater to small business customers—think Dell or UPS—routinely run contests that offer prizes of cash, equipment or services. Business schools often run seed money competitions for students or alums. New York University's Stern School of Business, for instance, each year hosts a Business Plan Competition, in which teams of students or alum vie for up to $175,000 in seed money, plus coaching, mentoring and feedback from seasoned entrepreneurs and investors.

Increasingly, online communities offer a way for a potential entrepreneur to find cash. Ideablob.com, for instance, runs an *American Idol*–style competition, inviting aspiring entrepreneurs to log on, trot their ideas out for all to see, and—if they garner enough votes from users—win $10,000 in seed money.

CHAPTER 4

ONCE YOUR FEET ARE WET

We've looked at how you can get your hands on the cash necessary to start your own business. But once you've been operating for a few years, you might need another round of cash—this time to expand or improve your business.

For instance, say your home-based business has really taken off. You've hired a few employees, you're regularly meeting with more clients—and now the space in your basement seems pretty tight. You dream of buying or leasing some nice office space, furnishing it to suit your tastes, wiring it for Internet access and installing new equipment.

Expansion into new locations or territories is generally the most common reason a small business might search out a business loan. An entrepreneur who's been in operation a few years might have other reasons to seek out financing, too—perhaps he or she wants to buy more inventory, upgrade equipment, renovate an existing facility or simply boost working capital.

Sometimes a growing business might have enough capital to fund an expansion or improvement outright. But the owner might seek out financing to ensure there's enough money on hand to cover any unexpected businesses expenses that arise. And of course, some business owners simply can't afford to lease new space or open another store unless they've got a loan. In that case, they're betting that the revenues generated by the expansion or improvement will cover the cost of the loan.

It's always a calculated risk to take on debt, so if you are considering it, you need to make sure the benefits are worth it. Maria Coyne, who administers KeyBank's SBA loan program in Cleveland, cautions that loans aren't for the unprepared: "If you lend someone money who's not ready for it, or who doesn't have a plan for it, then in many cases you are just hastening their failure." In other words, you'd better do your homework first.

It's best for entrepreneurs to educate themselves about the loan terms, payment options and interest rates, and to consult with others—such as an accountant, an attorney, a mentor or another business owner—who can offer advice about when and how much debt to take on. And it's critical to crunch the numbers to determine what you can afford when it comes to loan payments. If bookkeeping isn't your strength, hire someone who can help.

Here's a look at the various financing options available to small businesses, starting with the easiest (lines of credit) to the more difficult (sizable bank loans) to secure:

BUSINESS LINES OF CREDIT

A line of credit is possible to get as a new company, but it's far easier to secure when you're more established.

Business lines of credit work a lot like credit cards and help companies cover cash flow shortages and purchase big-ticket inventory. The amount you receive depends on past revenues and your ability to repay debt. For example, a bank might be willing to grant a small line of credit (in the range of $15,000 to $20,000) to a new business owner, largely on the strength of his or her personal credit score, but raise that amount to upward of $100,000 once the business grows.

HOW TO MAKE A LENDER SAY YES

Don't walk into your lender's office unprepared. The best candidates for a business loan are those who can show they're worth the money. Here are three important matters to reference:

1. *Your personal credit history.* Especially if your company has a short operating history, a lender will be keenly interested in your creditworthiness and ability to manage your personal finances.

2. *Your company's financial statements.* The best way to prove your company's sound health is to show a lender your detailed statements and projections. These documents also will demonstrate your financial skills.

3. *Your business plan.* It's like the famous job-interview question: "Where do you see yourself in five years?" Lenders want to see you've got a road map to success.

The most common line of credit is revolving, allowing a business owner to draw down (and replace) funds as needed, usually at a variable interest rate. The key to securing a line of credit is to show the bank you've got a handle on your cash flow and can repay those funds, according to Mark Hogan, who has served as president of small business banking at Bank of America in Charlotte, North Carolina.

"A true line of credit is a short-term bridge loan for working-capital needs," he says. "It's not intended for permanent working capital." A retail shop, for instance, might seek a line of credit to stock up on inventory before the Christmas rush; after the holiday season, the shop would pay off the balance using proceeds from sales.

To minimize the risk, many banks require a "cleanup" period in which the business maintains a zero balance on the line for thirty consecutive days at some point during the year.

Lines of credit are popular financing tools for small businesses, and helpful in establishing relationships with banks who can offer other types of financing (such as conventional loans) as needs arise.

MICROLOANS

A microloan, historically, is a small loan of less than $35,000 for a start-up or newly established company that doesn't yet qualify for a traditional business loan. Microlenders—often, nonprofit community groups—sometimes stipulate that business owners complete training or fulfill business planning requirements before funds are distributed.

For instance, the nonprofit Women's Venture Fund has lent more than $1.5 million in small loans to women entrepreneurs in New York and New Jersey since its inception in 1997. The group first helps female business owners beef up their financial and cash flow management skills, then provides loans in the range of a few thousand dollars to up to $25,000.

"We want to get to know them before we make commitments to them," says Maria Otero, Women's Venture Fund founder. "We don't want the funds to be used as a Band-Aid." A business owner who receives cash before she's ready often just digs herself deeper into a hole—something the group tries to prevent, Otero says.

Women's Venture Fund also makes loans to business owners whose poor credit histories make them unable to qualify for traditional bank loans. A typical applicant might be a business owner who's already running one retail shop and wants a loan to open a second shop but has been turned down because of a low credit score and her company's limited operation history, according to Otero. The group would work with the owner to improve her financial and business development skills, then award a loan for a specific purpose, such as the renovation of the second shop.

HOW DO I GET A MICROLOAN?

The application process will vary by lender, but let's take a look at Accion USA's process as an example. You can apply online at www.accionusa.org, and the application is generally processed within two to three weeks. Supporting documents you'll need include:

- A driver's license or passport

- Recent bank statements from your business and personal accounts

- A utility bill

- A detailed list of items you'd like to use as collateral, or a cosigner who will help guarantee the loan

- Your business plan (especially critical if your business has been in operation for less than twelve months)

Accion doesn't charge an application fee, but if your loan is approved, a service fee of between 4 percent and 6 percent will be folded into the loan amount. Accion USA offers loans up to $50,000, at terms of up to sixty months, at rates (in 2009) of 13 percent or higher.

Microloans have a few drawbacks, including the fact that their rates, in general, tend to be higher than those of standard business loans. And since microlenders often focus on particular communities, a business owner may have trouble finding a microlender in his or her area of the country. One place to search for a microlender is on the website of the industry trade group Association for Enterprise Opportunity, at www.microenterpriseworks.org.

Microloans may become more readily available as the microfiance movement continues to grow. In 2006, economist Muhammad Yunus won the Nobel Peace Prize for his work with Grameen Bank, an institution that provides tiny loans to entrepreneurs in impoverished countries. That awareness has led to more institutional and individual investments in U.S. microlenders. A big name in the microloan area is Accion USA, the Boston-based arm of the international lender Accion International, which has eight branches across the country. Since its founding in 2000, Accion USA has provided more than $26 million in loans to entrepreneurs, with more than 25 percent of new loans applied for online. (See the box "How Do I Get a Microloan?" on page 41.) Others include ACEnet in Athens, Ohio; Justine Petersen in St. Louis, Missouri; Mountain BizWorks in Asheville, North Carolina; Opportunity Fund in San Jose, California; and WESST Corp. in Albuquerque, New Mexico.

SBA LOANS

The government has a soft spot for the little guy, mostly because the country's twenty-seven million small businesses create about half of all private sector jobs and generate as much as 85 percent of all new jobs. The Small Business Administration guarantees loans such as the 7(a), Express and 504 products. The SBA doesn't actually lend the money, but rather guarantees up to 90 percent of its value, making it less risky for the real lender (usually a traditional bank) to grant the loan to a small business. In recent years, SBA loan volume has declined dramatically because of the banking crisis, although the economic stimulus package passed in early 2009 contained numerous provisions to revive small business lending.

SBA-guaranteed loans are particularly useful for companies that don't have a lot of fixed assets (such as property or equipment) that could serve as collateral. And typically, SBA loans have a longer maturity than a conventional bank loan— meaning payments are stretched out over longer terms (say, seven years versus five years), making it easier for a business owner to qualify.

But there are a lot of misconceptions when it comes to SBA loans. Many people mistakenly think they're grants (essentially, free money from the government) or for people with bad credit. "SBA is absolutely not a credit repair program," says Maria Coyne of KeyBank's SBA loan program. "You don't qualify for an SBA loan unless you've got strong personal credit."

In fact, a bank often places more weight on your personal credit history, as your business might not have enough of a track record or robust cash flow to meet traditional eligibility requirements, she says. And your character also is important— the bank typically runs FBI background checks on all applicants to make sure the information on your forms checks out.

To apply for an SBA loan, visit your local participating bank or financial institution. The nation's top banks, including Chase, Citibank, Bank of America, and Wells Fargo, all provide SBA loans, as do a growing number of credit unions. Lenders and borrowers can negotiate the interest rate, but the SBA sets maximum rates, which are pegged to the prime rate.

I asked Coyne to review each SBA loan type and who might apply. Here's a rundown:

7(A) LOAN

This basic loan—considered the SBA's flagship product—is named after section 7(a) of the Small Business Act, which authorized the agency to guarantee loans to the country's small businesses.

Under the 7(a) program, a business can apply for up to $2 million in financing; most companies at an early stage, however, usually qualify for a loan in the range of $150,000, says Coyne. The money is typically dispersed as a term loan with a fixed maturity and specified repayment schedule. A company with one to two years' worth of financial records might apply for a 7(a) loan to use for funding day-to-day operations, purchasing a building or equipment or machinery, or paying for a marketing or advertising campaign. "It's a very flexible, functional kind of loan product," she says. A lender will want to see a company's balance sheet, income statement and lists of receivables before granting the loan. New companies should be prepared to visit a banker with projections for growth and future revenues, too. "It's easier when the lender knows you have a road map," she says.

SBA Express

As the name implies, this program was designed with speed in mind: the average turnaround time is thirty-six hours. Business owners fill out a simplified, one-page application, and lenders make their decision largely on the strength of the owners' personal credit scores, Coyne says. One drawback is that less money is available—the maximum amount a small business owner can apply for is $350,000, and typical loan amounts usually fall in the range of $20,000 to $50,000. "It's a nice convenient product," she says, that's often used by new companies for working capital.

CDC/504

This program provides small businesses with long-term, fixed-rate financing (generally, up to $2 million) for purchases of fixed assets, such as land, buildings or equipment. So unlike 7(a) and SBA Express, the money can't be used for working capital. "It's a lesser known but very important program for the SBA," says Coyne. The SBA sponsors the program in conjunction with Certified Development Companies, or CDCs, which are nonprofit corporations chartered for a community's economic development. Under the program, a business would need to kick in 10 percent toward the purchase of the asset, but could receive up to 50 percent in financing from the bank or financial institution, and 40 percent from the CDC. The 504 program requires the borrower to create or retain one job for every $65,000 guaranteed by the SBA, with some exceptions. Businesses that apply for 504 loans are often in the manufacturing, construction or food production industries.

BANK LOANS

Ask any business owner and they'll tell you: requests for a bank loan often hit a dead end.

Usually, that's because companies ask for money long before they're ready. Keep in mind that conventional bank loans (say, $100,000 at a competitive rate) are usually only offered to businesses that can finance their growth without help from outside sources, such as guarantors. The worst candidate for a bank loan is a company that's struggling to pay its bills.

"A bank has to be repaid," says Rebecca Macieira-Kaufmann, executive vice president and head of the small business segment at Wells Fargo in San Francisco. "We're in one of the most highly regulated industries around. We can't be making loans if people can't repay them."

Do your homework before meeting with a banker or loan officer. Anticipate the types of questions you'll be asked; a thoroughly prepared borrower is much more likely to have his or her loan request approved. Remember, the bank doesn't want to give its money to someone who appears high-risk or lacks financial know-how. Get your documents in order, dress professionally and get ready to exude confidence at your meeting.

I asked Macieira-Kaufmann to outline what a bank looks at before giving a small business owner a loan. She says it's primarily the well-known 5 C's of lending—character, conditions, capital, capacity and collateral. Here's a summary of each:

- **Character.** "The bottom line is that a business, like a person, needs to take care of building a good credit history," she says. A bank wants to be assured that your company has paid its debts historically, whether that's supplier invoices, utility bills or even fees to the maker of your business cards. Keep records of all your payments to demonstrate your business credit profile, she suggests. Strong credit management is "the ground you walk on," she says. "That's character."

- **Conditions.** Why are you seeking a loan? Expect rejection if you need the money to bail out a sinking ship. Better reasons for needing a loan include opening a new office, upgrading equipment or expanding product lines. You need to show that the time is right to expand or improve and that your investment will reap profits. "Does it make sense where you are in your [company's] life cycle?" she says. "The use has to be logical." Be specific as to how much money you want, and be prepared to explain why that amount is needed.

- **Capital.** This is the equity that you personally put into the business. "Do you have skin in the game?" says Macieira-Kaufmann. Investing a considerable amount of your own money—not just other people's money—demonstrates your personal commitment to growing your company.

- **Capacity.** How do you plan to repay the loan? The bank wants to see that your business can generate enough cash flow from its operations to make loan payments. Essentially, "you have to have a profitable business," she says. Expect to show your banker two to three years of financial history, plus projected earnings for the years ahead.

- **Collateral.** In order to reduce its risk, a lender will want you to put up some form of security against the loan. That's a very traditional bank demand, says Macieira-Kaufmann, and usually comes in the form of real estate or company assets such as property or receivables.

One last C that many banks take into consideration is "customer"—are you a customer of the bank? Lenders prefer to work with business owners if they already know their history and financial behavior. If you have an existing business account or mortgage with the bank and have demonstrated your ability to pay bills and manage debts, then you're in a better position to have your loan request approved.

CHOOSING A BANK

Be choosy when it comes to selecting a bank. You want to find a financial institution that can grow with you over time. And it's not just about money: a good bank can provide you with support and assistance in the early years, and ultimately contribute to your long-term success. How to pick the right one?

- Ask successful entrepreneurs, or your lawyer or accountant, for referrals.

- Look for a bank that's familiar with your industry or understands the needs of emerging or growing companies.

- Seek out a bank that's active in small business lending, such as one that participates in the SBA's lending program.

- Check out the products and services the bank offers for small business owners, such as payroll services or online banking capabilities.

- Ask about investment products. As your company grows, you'll need a place to invest the company's profits, as well as your own.

A business owner often wants to work with a bank because he or she can secure large amounts of debt financing—that is, money that has to be repaid, usually with specific terms and rates—without having to give up any ownership interest or control to the lender.

In contrast, equity financing—that is, funds that an owner raises for the business, essentially by selling ownership stakes to outside parties—requires giving up a certain degree of control. In the chapters ahead, we'll take a look at angel investing and venture capital, and the role equity financing could play in your business.

CHAPTER 5

FINDING
AN ANGEL

If you're a cash-strapped entrepreneur looking for an infusion of capital, you may be curious about angel investors. Very few start-ups will receive an investment from an angel—in 2007, fewer than sixty thousand companies received angel funding, a relatively small figure considering more than ten times that many businesses are started each year. But for the right small business, this type of capital can fill the gap between that money you've gotten from friends and family and the venture capital (which we'll look at in the next chapter) that you hope to secure down the road.

So who is an angel exactly? An angel is a wealthy individual willing to invest in a company at its earlier stages in exchange for an ownership stake, often in the form of preferred stock or convertible debt. Angels are considered one of the oldest sources of capital for start-up entrepreneurs; the term itself, by most accounts, comes from the affluent patrons who used to finance Broadway plays in the early twentieth century. In 2007, angels invested $26 billion in 57,120 ventures, which breaks down to about $450,000 a deal, according to the Center for Venture Research at the University of New Hampshire in Durham. That makes angels a potentially powerful resource for newbie entrepreneurs with promising young companies.

But little is known or understood about the angel market, largely because it consists of individuals who make investments quietly. That is slowly changing, thanks in part to two organizations, the Angel Capital Association in Vienna, Virginia, which was founded in 2004, and its affiliate, the Angel Capital Education Foundation, which bring together angel groups to share best practices and provide basic information to entrepreneurs.

Whether you decide to seek an angel investment depends on your personal management style and the long-term plans for your company. Unlike a bank loan or other types of debt financing, equity capital (whether it's an angel investment or venture capital) gives someone else an ownership interest in your company. Many angels are successful entrepreneurs who have cashed out and now want to help others just starting out. While their expertise may be welcome, you need to ask yourself—especially if you're used to being in control—whether you want someone looking over your shoulder and making decisions for your company.

Keep in mind that an angel makes an investment in a high-risk opportunity (such as your fledging company) only when a return is expected. Angels typically look for "scalable" businesses that have the potential for great growth and a clear path toward profitability. In recent memory, angels (much like venture capitalists) have been attracted to hot start-ups in fields such as technology or life sciences, although increasingly angels are branching out into other sectors and in niche, mission-based areas. (See the box on page 51 for more on areas of interest to angels.)

If your business—say, a corner deli or gift shop—has no great plans to expand or enter new markets, an angel investor simply won't be interested. Because angels hope to make money by taking equity—usually preferred stock—in your company and realizing a large gain when the company is sold or goes public, they generally don't invest in "lifestyle" companies— that is, small consulting firms, local restaurants, retail shops or any businesses with limited earnings potential.

ANGELS WITH A MISSION

A growing number of angel or angel groups have a mission attached to their investment decision-making process. For instance, some groups are focusing on promoting economic development in a disadvantaged region, or helping a social or environmental cause. Other groups limit their funding to women- or minority-led businesses. The following angel groups are guided in their investing by various mission-based, nonfinancial objectives:

12 Angels
www.12angels.org
This Los Angeles group's mission is to create jobs and increase productivity for men and women recovering from alcoholism and addiction.

Phenomenelle Angels Fund
www.phenomenelleangels.com
This early-stage fund in Madison, Wisconsin, invests in women- and minority-owned or -managed businesses in Wisconsin and the Midwest.

Investors Circle
www.investorscircle.net
This San Francisco network focuses on small companies that address social and environmental issues, such as organic agriculture or sustainable forestry.

If your small business might help angels support a particular cause, look online for mission-based opportunities.

However, if you do have big plans for your company, angel financing might be for you.

I asked Susan Preston, author of *Angel Financing for Entrepreneurs* and an angel herself, to explain what an angel wants to see before making an investment. Here's her list:

- **A solid potential for return.** Angels want to know how your company will make money, when it will turn profitable, and when they can expect a return on their investment. You'll need to back up those promises of profitability with financial documents that include an income statement (also referred to as a profit/loss statement), a balance sheet and cash flow statements.

- **A good plan for the cash.** Investors want to make sure their money will be spent wisely. If you've founded, say, a consumer product company, you'll need to show how the money will be used to design, develop and distribute your product. And emphasize your thriftiness: angels don't want to see the money being used for big salaries or fancy office space.

- **A winning attitude.** Get fired up. Angels want to see passion; they want to see you're committed to your concept and company and that you'll stay the course when obstacles arise. Aside from enthusiasm, you must be able to clearly articulate your company's mission—and how you'll make that dream a reality.

- **A seasoned team.** Angels want to see a strong management team that's capable, experienced in their industry and, more important, open to suggestions and opinions. "If I don't think that a CEO or founder is coachable, I won't invest," Preston says. "Someone who comes in and says 'I know all the answers' is the kind of person who is doomed to failure."

- **A competitive edge.** How are customers responding to your product or service? An angel will want to know that you can capture market share quickly and beat out competitors as you ramp up. If your product or service is fairly unique, an angel will want to see you've secured the patents, copyrights or trademarks to protect your intellectual property.

- **A well-defined exit strategy.** Investors will want to know exactly how you plan to make them money—and just saying

"IPO" or "acquisition" might not be enough, Research how other companies in your industry have returned profits to investors. Identify potential suitors for your business. "It's a homework point that they need to have done," Preston says.

Of course, even after you've outlined your plan and all the reasons an angel should invest in your business, obtaining angel financing isn't easy. How do you find an angel?

The best way is through networking in your community. Seek out the right connections to potential investors by attending investment forums, small business education programs, business plan competitions and other events. It helps to stay local. With some exceptions, angels tend to invest close to home, as they want to coach you and keep tabs on their investment.

It's always a good idea to talk to other entrepreneurs who have gotten angel or venture backing and who can steer you in the right direction. Ask attorneys or accountants who deal in the private equity field for referrals. Research indicates that angels are more likely to invest in opportunities that have been recommended to them.

Angels often pool resources with other angels, forming angel groups or networks to minimize risks. Many groups have websites that outline their area of interest and investment criteria. Band of Angels in Menlo Park, California, for instance, says it invests in seed-stage high-tech companies with strong teams, proprietary technology and big markets. New World Angels, in Boca Raton, Florida, focuses on South Florida's early- and midstage companies. Silicon Pastures of Milwaukee looks for high-growth

ONLINE ANGELS

Your connection with an investor might only be a click away. More online tools are cropping up to match entrepreneurs with like-minded investors. Sites such as GoBigNetwork.com, RaiseCapital.com and FundingUniverse.com are specifically designed for small companies seeking a cash infusion. Many sites offer advice and allow entrepreneurs to post business plans and make e-mail or video pitches to investors.

HOW IS AN ANGEL DIFFERENT FROM A VENTURE CAPITALIST?

Venture capitalists generally don't provide seed or start-up financing, as angels do. VCs tend to get in later in the game, supplying high-growth companies with much larger chunks of financing—on average, more than $7 million a deal, according to the University of New Hampshire's Center for Venture Research.

Unlike angels, venture capitalists do not invest their own money—a common misconception. Instead, VCs typically invest money from institutions, such as big pension funds or college endowments, and, in some cases, high-net-worth individuals. VCs, because they have a fiduciary duty to maximize returns, typically demand board positions and veto rights to exert greater control over a company's direction. Angels, on the other hand, are more likely to play an advisory or mentoring role to a company's founder or principals.

Certainly, angels and VCs are alike in many ways. As professional investors, angels and VCs look to invest in companies in prosperous industries, and both have strict investment criteria: a venture needs to have a solid business plan, strong management team and viable exit strategy before it's considered for equity financing.

companies in Wisconsin's core industries of traditional manufacturing, high-tech and biotechnology. Most groups have information available online detailing how to apply for funds; be aware that some require an application fee (usually ranging between $100 and $250) to submit business plans.

For a start-up with outsized dreams, winning a deal with angels is often a precursor to bigger investments by venture capitalists, which we'll outline in the next chapter.

CHAPTER 6

Seeking
Venture
Capital

Venture capital, bottom line, is sophisticated money. It's reserved for innovative entrepreneurs who have dreamt up companies that have the potential for rapid, high-profit growth. Some prominent examples of venture-capital-backed companies include Microsoft, Intel, Google, Genentech and Medtronic, to name a few. In recent decades, entrepreneurs in hot industries such as technology, life sciences and biotechnology have secured funding from venture capitalists to ramp up their companies quickly, and with an eye toward going public or selling. Increasingly, entrepreneurs in fields such as renewable or "green" energy (including wind and solar power) are drawing the attention of forward-thinking VCs. However, for the average small business owner, venture capital is not likely to be an option, certainly not in the early years.

Venture capital (see the box "Venture Capital 101" on page 56) is often doled out to a company in multimillion-dollar rounds, over the course of several years. As discussed in the last chapter, venture capitalists typically don't invest seed or start-up capital, simply because the risk is too high. When the Internet bubble burst in 2000, a number of VC funds suffered disastrous losses because of investments in young start-ups that did not perform up to expectations. And with the recent economic downtown, VCs have become more prudent in their investments. In 2008, VCs invested $28.3 billion in 3,808 deals, the first yearly decline since 2003, according to the MoneyTree Report by PricewaterhouseCoopers and the National Venture Capital Association, based on data from Thompson Reuters. As a result, VCs are assessing each investment more carefully than ever, preferring companies that have the brightest outlook for the long term and can demonstrate on some scale that their business models are viable.

VENTURE CAPTIAL 101

Venture capital firms provide money and management experience in return for an ownership stake, usually in the form of preferred stock. Most firms pool money from institutions or individuals into an investment fund with a specific industry or regional focus. Money in the fund is dispersed to any number of start-up ventures so that investors can afford to lose money on some deals, but still profit if others perform well. VCs generally seek to exit investments within three to seven years.

If you're considering seeking venture capital for your company, you should understand that it's far more than just a pile of cash. Because of the large sums being invested—the average round is between $7 million and $8 million—venture capital partners take an active role in a company, sometimes managing day-to-day operations and taking board seats to exert control over a company's strategic direction. That type of outside control isn't for everyone, though.

To some entrepreneurs, VC is more like sacrilege than the holy grail. Take Kelly L. Roth, who was disgusted when her partners outvoted her and took $30 million in venture capital in the mid-1990s to grow their technology firm. Almost immediately, the investors installed a new chief executive, general counsel and in-house business manager for the company. "It was instant outside control," she recalls. While she had been driven by an enthusiasm for the business and a concern for employees, the investors cared only about taking the company public and exiting. Fed up with the new direction of the company, which now trades publicly on Nasdaq, she left about a year later.

Now running a defense contracting firm, Delta Solutions and Strategies in Colorado Springs, Colorado, Roth refuses to seek or take venture capital. Instead, she's working with a local bank and growing the company organically; in 2007, her revenues hit $9 million. She credits her fifty-member staff with much of the growth, and would like the company to be employee-owned someday. Does she recommend VC at all?

"Entrepreneurs need to fully understand the expectations of a venture capitalist," she cautions. "It is not a short-term fix but a long-term obligation." If the business is your passion and you want to direct its future, then venture capital is not for you, she warns.

Still, many entrepreneurs say they're willing to relinquish some control for a cash infusion.

Shoba Purushothaman, for instance, says venture capital allowed her to quickly build the NewsMarket, a free video service based in New York, into an international media company. After cofounding the company in 2000, she secured $3 million in early-stage financing in 2002, another round of $4 million in 2004 and a last round of $12.5 million in 2005.

The NewsMarket, which now has eighty-five employees and offices in San Francisco, London, Dubai, Mumbai and Beijing, "has grown revenues rapidly," she says. The money allowed her and her staff to build the company rather than constantly worry about where the next dollars would come from. And seasoned investors with media expertise and industry connections helped the company grow its corporate client base.

She advises other entrepreneurs to be selective and choose investors wisely. The "caliber and integrity of investors" are important to evaluate before you commit to a VC firm, she says. However, "I do believe the color of money is ultimately green," she says. "*Where* it comes from does not matter as much as the fact that it *is* coming."

Even if you feel venture capital is for you, you'll quickly find that it is exceedingly difficult to obtain. Venture capital firms have strict criteria for investment, and an entrepreneur needs to be thoroughly prepared if he or she wants to have any chance of winning financing. VCs want to see much the same checklist as angels do (outlined on page 52) but are even choosier, primarily because they're investing other people's money.

The process of selecting, pitching and ultimately negotiating with a VC can be intimidating, especially to those not accustomed to the world of high finance. I asked Lori Hoberman, who often represents entrepreneurs as chair of the venture and technology group at the law firm Fish and Richardson in New York, to explain the various steps. Here's what she said:

Pinpoint the ideal VC.

First, an entrepreneur must target the right venture capital investment fund to pitch. That requires some research. It's a good idea to attend venture capital and private equity conferences. Ask an attorney or accountant for a referral. Online databases such as VentureSource (owned by Dow Jones) provide information on the latest venture deals. And most VCs host websites that describe their "sweet spot" and existing portfolio investments, Hoberman says. Don't waste time pitching your biodiesel fuel business to a VC that only invests in software.

Prepare a "teaser" document.

This one- or two-page document that you send to VCs is your way of introducing yourself—and it's got to be memorable. Tell the VC who you are, what need you fill in the market and how that market translates into dollars. Because most VCs are barraged with investment requests and can give each one only limited consideration, every sentence of your teaser needs to "answer the question about why an investor would ever dream of putting money into you," Hoberman advises. "It forces you, as the entrepreneur, to think in sound bites." She recommends incorporating text and graphics (pictures, pie charts or graphs) into the document. "The whole idea is to tease the investor into wanting to hear more," she says.

Send financials.

If your teaser has done its job, a VC often will ask you to provide financial statements, including projections. If you're building out your business model and are attracting paying customers, "it's a much easier sell," says Hoberman. Show how you've gotten to your current stage, whether that's through bootstrapping, help from family and friends, or funding from angels.

Prepare your pitch.

If a VC wants a meeting after reviewing your financials, the initial face-to-face encounter will probably last less than a half hour, so use the time wisely. Don't forget the thirty-second rule, Hoberman advises. "You have to tell the investor in the first thirty seconds who you are and how you are going to make them money," she says. If you plan to show visuals, such as a slide show or online demonstration, keep it short so that there's time for questions. Demonstrate your belief in the company and your knowledge of the market or industry. "The VC wants to get a sense that you know what you are talking about," she says. When a company has more than one founder, it's also important for partners to demonstrate that they are a strong management team. "Look at each other when you talk, and show respect," she says.

Review the terms.

If your pitch was successful, you'll receive a term sheet for a first or "series A" round of financing (later rounds are called series B, series C and so on). The document outlines the deal that the VC is proposing before investing in your company. At

FIVE FACTS ABOUT VC

1. The top ten states for VC investment in 2007 were California, Massachusetts, Texas, Washington, New York, Pennsylvania, Maryland, Florida, New Jersey and North Carolina.

2. In the last thirty-five years, venture capitalists invested more than $441 billion in more than fity-seven thousand companies in the United States.

3. The clean technology sector, which includes alternative energy, pollution control and clean power supplies, has had the most venture capital investment growth in the last five years.

4. Since 1973, close to three thousand venture-backed companies have gone public on the U.S. stock exchanges. During that same period, more than four thousand venture-backed companies have been acquired for their innovations and business models.

5. The majority of venture capitalists were once entrepreneurs, scientists or engineers themselves before they began investing.

Source: National Venture Capital Association

that point, you and your advisors (specifically, an attorney who specializes in venture financing) should begin negotiations. The term sheet outlines voting rights, liquidation preferences and, more important, how much equity the VC will receive.

Figure out what you're worth.

In order to negotiate, you need to place a value on your company, which can be tough or imprecise at such a young stage. One approach is a so-called back-of-the-envelope valuation, which can be determined by deciding how much venture capital the company needs and how much equity you're willing to sell. "You try not to give away more than one-third of the company in the series A round," Hoberman says. For example, if you need $3 million in financing for your consumer product company but don't want to sell more than a one-third stake, you'd value your company (prior to receiving the capital) at $6 million.

Do your due diligence.
Before signing on the dotted line, take some time to consider the ramifications of your decision. Talk to other companies in the VC's portfolio about their experiences. Keep in mind that the VC will take board seats and expect progress reports at monthly meetings. Good VCs "understand the hills and valleys and can wait it out," Hoberman says. "The really bad ones ream the entrepreneur every time the slightest thing goes wrong."

CHAPTER 7

SPECIAL PROGRAMS FOR WOMEN AND MINORITIES

No book on small business would be complete without a special section on women and minorities (defined by the government and other sources as Hispanic, black, American Indian/Alaskan, Asian or Pacific Islander). That's because national statistics (see the box "Women Entrepreneurs" and "Minority Entrepreneurs" on page 64) show that women and minorities are embracing entrepreneurship in record numbers—a fact largely attributed to pay disparities, unequal treatment and lack of flexibility in the corporate world. Women who are raising children, in particular, often say they choose to start their own businesses to regain more control over their daily schedules and to find better balance in their work and family lives.

For many financial institutions, the dramatic rise of women and minority entrepreneurs has meant new business. Firms such

WOMEN ENTREPRENEURS

- Women-owned businesses have been growing in number at twice the rate of business overall for nearly two decades.

- Nearly 10.4 million firms are owned by women, employing more than 12.8 million people and generating $1.9 trillion in sales.

- Women-owned firms account for 41 percent of all privately held firms.

Source: Center for Women's Business Research

MINORITY ENTREPRENEURS

- Minority entrepreneurs are outpacing the national average. Between 1997 and 2002, the number of black-owned firms grew by 45 percent. Hispanic-owned businesses grew 31 percent. Asian-owned firms grew 24 percent. The national average for all businesses was 10 percent.

- Minorities own about 18 percent of the twenty-three million U.S. firms in 2002.

- The number of all minority-owned businesses increased 10 percent between 1997 and 2002.

- Hispanics or Latinos make up the largest minority business community, owning 6.6 percent of all U.S. firms.

- Firms vary by industry and race. For example, 16 percent of Native American–owned businesses were in construction; 20.5 percent of black-owned firms were in health care and social assistance; and Hispanic and Pacific Islander–owned businesses were concentrated in administrative, support, waste management and remediation (contaminant removal) services (13.2 percent and 11.6 percent, respectively).

Source: U.S. Small Business Administration, based on 2002 Census data

as Key, Wells Fargo and American Express have increased their investment in lending to women- and minority-owned business, viewing these historically overlooked segments as new clients for credit lines, cash management and investment services.

This new interest from financial institutions is creating better access to capital for women and minorities. It's important to note here that banks, by law, can't make decisions to lend based on someone's gender or race. Most financial institutions instead focus their marketing muscle on women and minority entrepreneurs, developing special programs, networking events and educational initiatives to target these new prospects. Often, the banks team up with women's business groups such as the National Association for Women Business Owners or minority networks such as the Hispanic Chamber of Commerce to sponsor seminars, roundtable discussions or large-scale conferences on various small business topics.

These extra efforts are needed. Let's look at history. It wasn't until 1974 that the Equal Credit Opportunity Act guaranteed access to credit and loans for women and minorities. Before that time, a single woman was often denied credit or forced to get a cosigner; married women had to take out loans in their husbands' names. Minorities in many communities were denied credit, even though they were fully qualified. Throughout the 1980s and 1990s, women and minority business owners still faced access-to-credit barriers.

What about today? The numbers indicate that obstacles still exist. Despite the impressive rates of starting up, women- and minority-owned businesses are not hitting the same revenue milestones as those owned by men and whites.

Let's take a look at the statistics. Less than 3 percent of women-owned businesses report $1 million or more in annual revenues, according to data from the Center for Women's Business Research. By comparison, more than twice that percentage of male-owned businesses take in $1 million or more. And in general, minority-owned businesses aren't doing as well as white-owned firms. On average, for every dollar that a white-owned firm made, Pacific Islander–owned firms made about 59 cents, Hispanic-, Native American– and Asian-owned businesses made 56 cents, and black-owned businesses made 43 cents, according to a 2007 SBA report.

What's holding women and minorities back? The answer appears to be twofold. Much has been written about the importance of role models; many women (especially those considered baby boomers or Generation X) say they had hardworking fathers but weren't exposed to successful female business leaders in their early years. Similarly, minorities who grew up under challenging circumstances say they had few sources of inspiration within their own communities. And both women and minorities say they continue to be dogged by stereotypes that they lack business savvy and financial know-how.

Christina Vitagliano, for instance, says she's frustrated by the subtle (and sometimes blatant) unequal treatment that she's receiving, particularly as her company grows more prosperous. A veteran of the marketing industry, Vitagliano opened an antiques business in 1998, which she grew successfully and sold in 2003. In 2004, she launched a new company, a family-friendly, glow-in-the-dark, indoor minigolf concept called Monster Mini Golf. Her husband, Patrick, who had a background in theatrical production, soon joined her in the business, and the two have turned the company into a franchise with more than twenty locations.

But the bigger the company grows, the more suppliers, vendors, customers and potential franchisees and investors ask to speak with Patrick—even though the company was her idea and she handles much of its management. "They say, 'Can we talk to the guy?'" Christina says. "They've now decided, 'Oh, since it's that big, it must be Patrick.' People have actually said to me, 'There is no way you could have done that.'"

So by agreement, Patrick often takes the phone calls and does the talking—then hangs up the phone and runs everything by Christina. "It's very *Remington Steele*," she says, referring to the 1980s show in which a female private detective establishes a fictitious male identity so she can be taken seriously. "It is still a man's world," Christina says. "That is deflating when you are working a million hours a week."

Another business owner, Judi Henderson-Townsend, found she likewise had to navigate the waters delicately to build her business. On a whim, back in 2001, Henderson-Townsend bought the inventory of a San Francisco Bay–area mannequin rental shop that was going out of business. She bought fifty mannequins, launched MannequinMadness.com to buy and sell more, and soon had a stock of more than a thousand torsos and life-sized body forms, mostly in her garage and backyard.

Henderson-Townsend likes to joke that she had the "triple whammy" when she started Mannequin Madness. Not only was she in a unique industry without many success stories to imitate, but she's also a woman and an African American. When she first designed her website, she made a conscious decision not to reveal her race or gender to potential customers. Customers buying online didn't need any more reasons to fear that she couldn't deliver, she reasoned.

Henderson-Townsend has felt more comfortable revealing her identity since she's garnered a few accolades, posting photos of herself and news articles on her site. She's won Wells Fargo's Living History award for African American entrepreneurs, a $100,000 grant from an Intel-sponsored technology contest and a special achievement award from the Environmental Protection Agency for her recycling efforts. She's moved her dummies into a warehouse, opened up another location in New York and plans to expand to Los Angeles.

Henderson-Townsend has taken advantage of special programs offered by banks, minority networks, business groups and universities to learn more about financing and basic business principles, such as inventory and cash flow management. The education has been critical to her success, she says. "A lot of times, people of color haven't had people in their family, or a neighbor, who have been business owners," she says. "Many times, we don't have the role models."

She's found it interesting—and in many ways, inspirational—to attend seminars and classes with white businessmen. "Men have greater risk tolerance and can burn through money," she says. "Many times, minorities don't have the option to do that—there's just more at stake." Also, she's noticed that the men in her classes seem to handle failure better than women often do, not dwelling on it and simply moving on to the next project. "Women will personalize it," she says. "If you fail, it's 'I'm not a good businessperson.'"

That's led her to a basic conclusion. "Both minorities and women have to free up our mind-set," she says, "because we haven't been in the game long enough."

RESOURCES FOR WOMEN AND MINORITIES

When it comes to growing a business—whether that's learning the basics or securing capital—these places can offer assistance to traditionally underserved small business owners and entrepreneurs.

FINANCIAL INSTITUTIONS

Many financial institutions have special programs or services designed to teach women or minority entrepreneurs about funding options. You can usually learn more about them on their websites. Here are a few to check out:

KeyBank—Key4Women
www.key.com/html/I-5.html
Key began focusing on female entrepreneurs as their ranks grew, setting a lending goal in 2005 of $1 billion to women business owners over a three-year period. By 2007, that goal had been surpassed and the bank now aims to lend $2 billion

to women business owners over the next five years. The bank's Key4Women program, for women who bank with Key, offers educational programs, a newsletter and networking events. In 2008, the bank launched a Key4Women Resource Center in Albany, New York, to provide a comfortable space where women entrepreneurs can meet, network and find resources.

Wells Fargo—Women/Diverse Business Services

www.wellsfargo.com/biz/women_diverse_business
Wells Fargo has lending goals for women, African-American, Asian and Latino business owners, and provides information, advice, resources and support through financial education and community outreach. The bank also has special services for disabled business owners, as well as lesbian, gay, bisexual and/or transgender entrepreneurs.

American Express—Women's Business Initiative from OPEN

www133.americanexpress.com/osbn/wbi/index.asp
American Express focuses on women business owners through this initiative, offering a book series, teleconferences and online tools designed for women entrepreneurs. AmEx also partners with national organizations (most notably, Count-Me-In, for the Make Mine a Million program; see more on page 71, under "Nonprofits") to provide money, mentoring and marketing to women business owners.

GOVERNMENT

Women's Business Centers of the Small Business Administration

www.sba.gov/aboutsba/sbaprograms/onlinewbc/index.html
More than a hundred centers throughout the United States help women start and grow small businesses by providing training in finance, management, marketing, procurement and other areas.

National Women's Business Council

www.nwbc.gov

The council's mission is to promote initiatives, policies and programs that support women-owned companies at all stages of development in the public and private sector marketplaces.

WomenBiz.gov

www.womenbiz.gov/

This site, sponsored by the National Women's Business Council, is designed to teach female entrepreneurs how to bid on government contracts. The federal government spent $11.6 billion with women-owned small businesses in 2006, according to the council.

SBA's 8(a) and SDB Business Development

www.sba.gov/aboutsba/sbaprograms/8abd/index.html

The SBA administers two programs for what it terms "socially and economically disadvantaged" businesses. Members of certain minority groups automatically qualify; business owners who are socially disadvantaged because of ethnicity, gender, physical handicap or location may also qualify. To be considered economically disadvantaged, individuals must have a net worth of less than $250,000, excluding the value of the business and personal residence. The 8(a) Business Development Program offers a broad scope of assistance to socially and economically disadvantaged firms, while the Small Disadvantaged Business Certification Program pertains to benefits in federal procurement.

U.S. Department of Commerce Minority Business Development Agency

www.mbda.gov

The Minority Business Development Agency is the only federal agency created specifically to foster the establishment and growth of minority-owned businesses in the United States. The agency's programs focus primarily on access to capital and market opportunities for minority entrepreneurs.

Nonprofits

Springboard Enterprises

www.springboardenterprises.org

This nonprofit out of Washington, D.C., is dedicated to accelerating women's access to the equity markets. The group produces programs that educate, showcase and support female entrepreneurs as they seek equity capital and grow their companies.

Make Mine a Million

www.makemineamillion.org/site

As the name might indicate, this program has a chief goal: to help women-owned businesses surpass the million-dollar revenue mark. The annual program selects women entrepreneurs from around the United States to receive money, mentoring and marketing opportunities. Candidates are narrowed down through contests sponsored by the nonprofit Count-Me-In and American Express's small business division, OPEN.

National Minority Business Council

www.nmbc.org

Founded in 1972, the National Minority Business Council says it knows what its members want: better access to capital and more sales. The council provides a range of services (including contract procurement announcements and an IPO prep course) to minority- and women-owned business enterprises.

Educational Institutions

Many business schools offer special programs, courses or executive education for women or minority entrepreneurs. Here's a look at three. Check websites of schools in your area for more local opportunities.

University of California at Los Angeles—Anderson Leadership Suite

www.anderson.ucla.edu/x18077.xml

UCLA's business school teaches special managerial and lead-

BARRIERS TO GROWTH?

Women still lag behind men when it comes to securing outside capital to grow their businesses. While the use of commercial credit by women-owned businesses grew 67 percent between 1996 and 2003, female entrepreneurs are still less likely to use debt or equity financing to grow their business.

- 71 percent of women business owners don't consider using equity capital, such as money from angel investors or VCs

- 51 percent don't consider using unsecured personal loans

- 23 percent have never sought a business bank loan

- 19 percent have never sought a business line of credit

Source: Center for Women's Business Research

ership skills to executive participants who are women, African American, Latino, lesbian, gay, bisexual or transgender.

Dartmouth University's Tuck Minority Business Programs
www.tuck.dartmouth.edu/exec/targeted_audiences/minority.html
For more than twenty-five years, Tuck has provided minority business executive programs, including "Building a High-Performing Minority Business" and "Growing the Minority Business to Scale."

Babson College's Center for Women's Leadership
www3.babson.edu/CWL/whatwedo/professionals.cfm
Babson's Center for Women's Leadership collaborates with the college's executive education program to offer special courses on leadership development for female entrepreneurs and other business professionals.

CHAPTER 8

ORGANIC GROWTH STRATEGIES

I n earlier chapters, we looked at how a business can fuel its growth by taking on investors as part of a larger plan to be acquired or go public. In this chapter, I'll discuss organic growth without outside investment—that is, the slower, steadier process by which a business can expand by increasing sales, providing more products or services and operating in the most efficient manner possible. Indeed, the majority of small businesses will grow in this fashion, in part because the business itself isn't suitable for angel or venture financing. But even if it is, many entrepreneurs decide to forgo investors in order to maintain a level of control over the "baby" they've raised. For those entrepreneurs, shepherding a company's growth slowly over time can be just as rewarding as rapidly securing profits with the help of outside investors.

Native Angels is one of my favorite examples of a company thriving though this organic growth. This homegrown health care agency was launched in 2000 by two entrepreneurial sisters, Bobbie Jacobs-Ghaffar, forty-one, and Lesa Jacobs, forty-three, with only a cell phone, two patients, and one nursing

ABOUT BOOTSTRAPPING

When you start a company with little money and no outside funding—carefully monitoring expenses while you're growing—your growth model is often referred to as "bootstrapping." Another definition of bootstrapping? Quite simply, doing more with less.

Some entrepreneurs bootstrap companies and then grow them organically, in the hope they'll eventually be able to secure external capital. Take Genevieve Thiers, who wanted to start a company called Sittercity to help people find babysitters through an online database. When she pitched Sittercity to investors in 2001, she was told: "We don't fund babysitting clubs." That meant she needed to bootstrap. After borrowing $120 from her dad to buy the Sittercity.com domain name, Thiers kept her overhead low by doing much of the dirty work herself. She distributed twenty thousand flyers though the city of Boston on foot, chased moms down in supermarkets and recruited sitters on college campuses. As the business grew, she reinvested profits, expanding into pet-sitting and house-sitting. Now she employs thirty-two people and serves individuals and corporate clients in cities throughout the United States. The bootstrapping has finally made investors interested: in 2008, her company closed on its first round of series A financing to fuel more domestic growth.

Other entrepreneurs choose to bootstrap because they want more freedom to develop the company as they see fit. "Having no investors has allowed us to protect our own culture and grow at our own pace," says Paul Spiegelman, who bootstrapped Beryl Companies, a health care call center in the Dallas–Fort Worth area, which he started in 1985 with his two brothers. Beryl now employs three hundred people and posts revenues of $30 million. If you're forced to bootstrap out of economic necessity, look at the benefits, he suggests. "It gives you total control over your destiny, and allows you to grow without outside stakeholders putting pressure on you."

assistant. Today, Native Angels employs 420 people, provides care to 850 patients a day, and posts about $12 million in annual revenues. Remarkably, the sisters built the business almost entirely through bootstrapping (see the box "About Bootstrapping" on page 74), rarely relying on loans or any type of outside investment. In the early days, they stretched their meager cash resources, even maxing out personal credit cards at one point. (As covered in Chapter 3, using personal credit cards to fund a start-up can be a dangerous strategy, as you can easily rack up debt; if you do use plastic, a better plan is to use it for a limited number of expenses that can be paid back quickly.) But they relied most heavily on their biggest strengths: a deep knowledge of the community they wanted to serve, a passion for the work they were doing and a can-do attitude inspired by growing up with very little.

Both sisters are members of the Lumbee Indian Tribe and treat the rural population throughout North Carolina's Robeson County. Many of their patients are low income and, like themselves, Lumbee Indians. The area has long been plagued by drugs, racism and poverty—per capita income hovers around $13,000. Illiteracy is rampant. It wouldn't appear to be an area where a business could grow, let alone flourish.

The sisters were inspired to reach out to the community and start Native Angels when, in quick succession, they lost two aunts to lung cancer. One aunt was treated at a hospital, where up until her final days the routine, cure-focused care included chemotherapy and radiation. She died in pain, at the hospital. But the other aunt was able to die at home, in a far more comfortable setting, and the sisters were able to spend quality time with her at the end.

Witnessing the difference in these two end-of-life experiences gave them a clear mission: create a business that would provide home health care to patients who are elderly, disabled, chronically or terminally ill or recuperating from acute illness. And beyond health care, the sisters wanted to empower residents of Robeson County—especially those living in poor economic conditions—to make informed decisions about their health care.

The two took a leap of faith in 2000, with Jacobs-Ghaffar exhausting two credit cards to start the home-based business. Without money to advertise, they enlisted volunteers to spread the word about Native Angels' services throughout their tight-knit community. Soon they had sixty patients, and within three months they had moved into an office and hired a small field staff. The company turned a profit in its first year, and the sisters reinvested those profits, expanding services to offer mental health counseling, hospice and early intervention for children with developmental disabilities. They set up Native Angels to accept Medicaid (the largest program for people who can't afford to pay for health care), Medicare, military insurance, private insurance and cash. By the end of 2006, the company was posting $11 million in revenue—a track record so robust that the Small Business Administration named the sisters Small Business Persons of the Year, honoring their achievements at a ceremony in Washington, D.C.

In 2007, the company took on debt for the first time in its history, taking out an SBA 504 loan to build a new $7.2 million headquarters. The 36,000-square-foot-facility, in Pembroke, North Carolina, now hosts Native Angels' corporate headquarters as well as an urgent care center, a full-service cafeteria, a gift shop and florist, a pharmacy, a full-service spa and a chapel. Part of the facility is commercial office space that can be leased. The sisters also have created a foundation, Angel Elite, to sponsor youth athletic teams, with a particular focus on building self-esteem in girls through sports, and are planning to build a nonprofit sports complex in coming years.

I asked Jacobs-Ghaffar to outline how the sisters grew Native Angels, organically and profitably, so that other entrepreneurs might learn from their experience. The tips she provided are most suited to business owners who are past the start-up phase and intent on growing (or turning around) their business. Here is her advice:

Don't forget your original goals.

Especially as the years go by, "stay true to your mission, and your vision," she says. To this day, Jacobs-Ghaffar still goes to patients' homes to remind herself of the work her company does and the population it serves. While private equity investors have sought to buy her company, or divisions of it, she has steadfastly refused to sell. "It's not about making money," she says. "That's not why I started, and that's not what keeps me in business."

Maintain that fighting spirit.

"You have to keep the same attitude that you had when you started," she says. When you're starting out, you hustle. When challenges arise—and they certainly will—you need to attack them with the same tenacity you did in the early days. Even when you have teams of employees, as the owner, you need to be involved in your company's operations and take care of problems yourself.

Surround yourself with good people.

Native Angels employs registered nurses, social workers, counselors, child care specialists, physical therapists and chaplains. Jacobs-Ghaffar credits much of the company's success to her staff; she trusts them to do their jobs with integrity and adhere to Native Angels' ethical code of "means, methods and morals." It's also important to hire people, especially at the management level, who will offer viewpoints and perspectives that are different from your own. "Surround yourself with people who will challenge you, and not just tell you want you want to hear," she says.

Get expert advice, but be the decision maker.

Certainly, you need to rely on advice from accountants, lawyers and tax experts. But remember, "you can't completely turn everything over to them," she says. Be centrally involved in any financial or legal decision made by your company. Most important, understand how cash flows into and out of your business. Know what your operating budget is and how much you can afford to invest in improvements or future projects. "It's really pretty simple. When it's your own business, it's your own money," she says.

Come up with a strategic plan.

Jacobs-Ghaffar didn't have a business plan when she started up. As time went on, she realized the problem with that. Not only did she not have clear goals, but she also had no way to measure the progress Native Angels was making. After three years in business, she sought help from the Small Business Technology and Development Center, a partnership between the University of North Carolina and SBA, which provides help to entrepreneurs. Working with four counselors from the SBTDC, she and her core managers spent three days away from the office, mapping out a five-year strategic plan. "We talked about long-term and short-term goals," she says. "We just got out big markers and wrote everything out." The plan has helped Native Angels hit target revenues and patient numbers and offer a variety of new services, she says. Now, she and her managers meet weekly to talk over ideas and chart their progress.

Build a reputation.

When starting out, the two sisters knew that to win patients, they had to win respect in their community via a grassroots approach. They spoke to members of churches, met with non-profits and hosted free clinics. "We got people in the community to buy into our vision," Jacobs-Ghaffar says. "When you get people to do that, you can do amazing things." More important, they also listened to what people told them, which is why they expanded into mental health and other services. Business owners in different industries will use a variety of methods to create a positive presence in the marketplace, such as speaking at educational events or business programs, or throwing

AVOIDING COMMON MISTAKES

While Native Angels was able to expand successfully, some businesses stumble during the growth phase, losing time and money in the process. I asked an expert, Bruce Judson, senior faculty fellow at the Yale School of Management, about how to avoid common pitfalls.

The biggest mistake most business owners make, he says, is assuming you need limitless financial resources to expand. In fact, it's more critical than ever to run a lean operation while simultaneously expanding. How to do that? Quite simply: Don't try to sell something no one wants to buy. Don't overpay for technology. Don't blow your budget by hiring staff you don't need. Judson, author of *Go It Alone*, about building successful enterprises with minimal investment, expands on these three points below:

- *Don't dive in without testing your great idea.* Will customers spend money on your new product or service? As you develop business ideas, see if you can find people who aren't already personally or professionally connected to you who think it's a good idea, too. Figure out a low-cost way to test-market your idea to reduce the possibility of failure, he says. And don't be afraid to tweak your ideas based on your findings.

- *Choose inexpensive, easy-to-use technology.* Don't waste money buying products that will soon be outdated, or paying programmers to develop specialty software for your business, he says. Instead, take advantage of hosted software, or software as a service (SasS), which many companies use to beef up sales and marketing efforts. Generally, for a monthly fee, you get access to the Internet-based services, which are maintained and updated by the SaaS providers (see Chapter 12 on technology).

- *Try outsourcing as an alternative to hiring staff.* This doesn't mean sending jobs or functions out of the country. Instead, figure out what you do best, and then hand off other work to freelancers, consultants or virtual assistants, who are generally far less expensive than employees (see page 146). "The more you can keep your overhead down, the better off you are," he says.

workshops or open houses. Native Angels also has built its reputation through its philanthropic work.

Keep a journal, especially when things aren't going well.

When your business is facing a challenge, write about the problem that's occurring—with updates on how you're resolving the issue. This strategy has been very effective for Jacobs-Ghaffar through the years; the written history is invaluable, especially when a new difficult situation arises. "I will go back and look at some problem that we had, and I'll see that we handled it and came out okay," she says. "I will look at what words of wisdom I consulted that day." She also keeps track of milestones, too, for inspiration.

Don't be intimidated by size.

Can you serve one customer? Then you can serve ten. Can you manage a few dollars? Then you can manage thousands. "Take the small things and extrapolate that into larger things," she says. Some companies can't grow because the owner can't imagine hiring that many workers or taking on such large projects. But Jacobs-Ghaffar emphasizes that the skills that have led you to accomplishments thus far are the basic abilities that you need to grow. Have faith in yourself, maintain those best practices and keep your eyes on the goal, she says.

Now that she's been successful in business, Jacobs-Ghaffar is turning more attention to her nonprofit work—the best reward of all, in her estimation. Simply put, "you can take your money and create things that help other people," she says.

CHAPTER 9

Handling Your Company's Finances

Many people start a business because they want to support themselves doing what they love. Too often, though, they neglect to focus on the numbers side of the business. Creative types, especially, often say they're turned off by the "unappealing," "complicated" or "just plain boring" aspect of financial management.

If you want to be successful, you'll need to ramp up your accounting knowledge. While you can certainly rely on an accountant, bookkeeper, or trusted employee to provide advice on your company's finances, it's critical that you gain a comfortable understanding of the numbers. As the owner, you'll need to make important decisions concerning the purchase of inventory or equipment, expansion into new markets or the hiring of more employees. To do so, you'll need to have a handle on your company's finances.

Consider these words from an accountant who advises business owners in New Zealand: "You can't change the past but you can usually influence the future." When times are tough, you'll want to know where every penny is going so you can figure out where to cut or reduce future spending. And when business is booming, you'll want to be able to track your progress, too.

HOW ONE BUSINESS OWNER CONQUERED THE NUMBERS

Wendy Goldstein's story is like that of many entrepreneurs: she wanted to turn her passion into a business. After graduating from Ohio State with a degree in fashion merchandising, Goldstein opened up Costume Specialists in 1981, selling custom-made costumes to corporations, schools and theater companies. Goldstein, who knew little about accounting or finance, served as the creative force behind the Columbus, Ohio, company, while her husband managed the books.

About ten years later, Goldstein's personal life suffered a blow as she and her husband decided to go their separate ways. And just as devastating, Costume Specialists had sunk deep into debt, despite $600,000 in annual revenues. During the divorce, Goldstein had to decide whether to fold the floundering business (her husband wasn't interested in keeping it) and declare bankruptcy or try to salvage what was left. "I just remember standing in front of the window, crying my eyes out," she remembers. "This was my passion. I thought I was going to lose the whole thing." That's when she had her aha moment, thinking: "Excuse me, but goddamn it, I worked so hard, I am not going to lose it now!"

Goldstein rolled her sleeves up and got to work. First priority? Getting to know her company's finances—something she'd made the mistake of never doing before. At the time, she had an eighteen-year-old college student working part-time on the books. She called him into her office and said, "Okay, I need to know every Friday these three things: how much money we have in the bank, how much people owe me and how much I owe people." She remembers him laughing and saying, "You mean you want cash flow, accounts receivable and accounts payable." Her response was: "I don't care what you call it. I just need to know it!"

Today, nearly two decades later, Goldstein still gets those reports every Friday. And the company that was on the brink of collapse now makes $2.8 million in annual revenues, employs forty-one people and has four different divisions, including a retail shop and a custom cleaning-and-storage business.

Goldstein credits much of the company's success to her ability to read financial statements. Aside from working with her bookkeeper, she took classes and workshops, many offered by the Small Business Administration, on basic financial management, and she peppered her banker with questions every time she had a meeting. She got the company out of debt by listing each creditor, starting with the ones that had the highest interest rates or penalties. Then she made a list of all of the company's expenses, figuring out areas where she could save money—even if it was only $10—and use it to pay off debt. "We just had to figure out how to whittle it away," she says. "We did it in little bits."

Goldstein eventually moved her handwritten system onto QuickBooks, a popular accounting software. She reviews her balance sheet and profit-and-loss statement on a quarterly basis, and her receivables, payables and cash flow reports weekly. In 2001, she was able to diversify her client base by purchasing a company that makes inflatable costumes (think Michelin Man) for $7 million.

When the economy melted in September 2008, Goldstein says good record keeping allowed her to methodically strip away expenses rather than panic. To cope with a 50 percent drop in income from her costume manufacturing business, Goldstein scanned the reports, calculated she'd need to cut $40,000 to $50,000 in expenses a month, then started slashing where she could. She immediately stopped paying for employees' parking (a small but costly perk) and renegotiated contracts to save on shipping costs. She switched her employees to health savings accounts from more costly traditional health insurance plans. Needing to save more, she reduced employees' salaries by 10 percent and laid off seven people—a painful but necessary decision. Having an intimate knowledge of your company finances "is huge," she says. "It allows you to react quickly."

Goldstein says she shocked herself because she'd never thought she'd have the accounting skills to run a business. "I still can't believe I figured it out," she laughs. But it's allowed her to continue doing what she loves, nearly thirty years after starting up.

THE BASICS

Let's take a look at the basic financial statements that every business owner should prepare and review on a regular basis: the profit-and-loss statement, the balance sheet and the cash flow statement. I asked Libby Ladu, founder of Right Brain Ventures and a financial advisor to entrepreneurs, to describe how each of these statements can help you understand your company's overall performance and health. Check out sample financial statements on the following pages.

Profit-and-loss statement.

This is a historical record (also known as an income statement) that shows how much you've made in revenues, how much you've spent and what your net income is over a specific period of time. The time period could be a week, a month, a quarter or a year, although monthly is the most common, Ladu says. The P&L tells you whether or not you're making money, and how much you're either making or losing. A further benefit: if structured properly, the P&L can show you which products or services are selling the best and where you are spending too much on expenses ranging from office personnel to advertising.

SAMPLE FINANCIAL STATEMENTS

Everything for Everyone, Inc.

PROFIT & LOSS STATEMENT
for the year ending December 31,

	2008
Sales	
Product #1	$550,000
Product #2	225,000
Total Sales	**$775,000**
Cost of Goods Sold	333,000
Gross Profit	**$442,000**
Operating Expenses	
Sales & Marketing Expense	
Advertising	43,000
Promotion/Marketing	6,500
Commissions	23,000
Total Sales & Marketing Expense	72,500
General & Administrative Expense	
Payroll & Payroll Taxes—excl. Officer	98,500
Payroll & Payroll Taxes—Officer	35,000
Rent & Utilities	18,000
Depreciation & Amortization	4,000
Telecommunication/Internet	36,000
Equipment & Supplies	25,000
Maintenance & Repairs	6,250
Postage & Delivery	3,450
Travel & Entertainment	7,800
Professional Fees (Legal/Accounting)	12,000
Other Office Expenses	6,500
Total General & Administrative Expense	252,500
Total Operating Expenses	325,000
Operating Profit	117,000
Other Income/(Expense)	
Net Interest Income/(Expense)	(4,200)
Other Income/Expense	0
Total Other Income/(Expense)	(4,200)
Profit Before Taxes	112,800
Taxes	67,000
Net Profit	**$45,800**

Source: Libby Ladu, president and founder, Right Brain Ventures, LLC

SAMPLE FINANCIAL STATEMENTS

Everything for Everyone, Inc.

BALANCE SHEET
as of December 31,

	2007	2008
ASSETS		
Current Assets		
Bank Accounts		
Checking Account #1	$24,000	$73,800
Checking Account #2	4,500	4,500
Accounts Receivable	91,000	111,000
Inventory	74,500	60,000
Prepaid Expenses	1,450	1,450
Total Current Assets	195,450	250,750
Fixed Assets		
Machinery & Equipment, Gross	38,600	83,600
Accumulated Depreciation	(16,000)	(20,000)
Net Machinery & Equipment	22,600	63,600
Other Assets	1,250	1,250
Total Assets	**$219,300**	**$315,600**
LIABILITIES & EQUITY		
Liabilities		
Current Liabilities		
Accounts Payable	$35,000	$52,000
Credit Card #1	34,000	24,000
Credit Card #2	6,500	5,000
Other Current Liabilities	0	0
Total Current Liabilities	75,500	81,000
Long-Term Liabilities		
Bank Loan #1	20,000	65,000
Total Long-Term Liabilities	20,000	65,000
Total Liabilities	95,500	146,000
Equity		
Paid in Capital	5,000	5,000
Retained Earnings	65,800	118,800
Net Income	53,000	45,800
Total Equity	123,800	169,600
TOTAL LIABILITIES & EQUITY	**$219,300**	**$315,600**

Source: Libby Ladu, president and founder, Right Brain Ventures, LLC

Balance sheet.

This is a snapshot of your company's financial health, providing a summary of your company's assets, liabilities and net worth. In other words, the balance sheet (sometimes called the statement of financial condition) tells you what you own and what you owe, Ladu says. Your assets will be the resources that your business controls: cash, equipment, buildings, furniture and money owed to you. Your liabilities will be the debts or other obligations that you owe others, such as accounts payable, taxes, loans and payroll. Your net worth (also known as equity) is what's left over—or assets minus liabilities.

Cash flow statement.

This captures how cash has flowed in and out of your company over a specific period of time. Think of it like the ledger of your personal checkbook, which shows money coming in, money going out and the remaining balance. "The cash flow statement is a very important financial statement because even though your P&L may be showing a profit, the business may not be generating cash," Ladu says. "And the reverse is also true." For instance, your sales may be growing as billings increase to new customers, but your new customers may be slow to pay, she says. At the same time, you might be spending more on inventory in anticipation of growth. The cash flow statement will show how all those changes affect your cash position.

Many business owners, such as Wendy Goldstein in our example, rely on financial software such as QuickBooks, MYOB, Peachtree or Microsoft Office to keep good records of all expenses and revenues. Other use more basic Excel spreadsheets. Before you invest, consult any number of online forums (www.cnet.com is one) to hear what other business owners like or dislike about the programs.

CASH FLOW PROJECTIONS

Because cash flow is the lifeblood of any business, we'll take a closer look here on how to make long-term projections about

SAMPLE FINANCIAL STATEMENTS

Everything for Everyone, Inc.

CASH FLOW STATEMENT
as of year ending December 31, | **2008**

OPERATING ACTIVITIES	
Net Profit	$45,800
Adjustments to Reconcile Net Income to	
Net Cash Provided by Operations:	
Depreciation	4,000
Decrease/(Increase) in Inventory	14,500
Increase/(Decrease) in accounts Payable	17,000
Decrease/(Increase) in Accounts Receivable	(20,000)
Net Cash Provided by Operating Activities	$61,300
INVESTING ACTIVITIES	
Purchase of Production Machinery	(45,000)
Net Cash Provided by Investing Activities	($45,000)
FINANCING ACTIVITIES	
Decrease in Credit Card #1	(10,000)
Decrease in Credit Card #2	(1,500)
Increase in Term Loan	45,000
Net Cash Provided by Financing Activities	$33,500
Net Cash Increase for Period	$49,800
Net Cash at Beginning of Period	$28,500
Cash at End of Period	**$78,300**

Source: Libby Ladu, president and founder, Right Brain Ventures, LLC

your company's finances. Understanding how money moves in and out of your company will help you measure the amount of cash you have on hand—and prepare you for any surpluses or shortages down the road.

Projecting your cash flow is a bit like preparing your budget and balancing your checkbook at the same time. You'll begin with a starting point—say, the first of the year—and then you'll outline your anticipated income and expenditures for the next several months or year. Be careful about assuming too much—and don't forget to factor in everything from insurance payments to raises in employees' salaries.

Keep in mind, to be most effective, cash flow projections should be updated on a regular basis with the most accurate numbers. For instance, a customer who's been reliable in the past might suddenly flake on paying. Or a vendor might decide to raise prices or tack on extra fees. Plugging in that new data will help you predict any cash crunches that might arise as a result.

I asked Jerry L. Mills, founder of B2B CFO, a Phoenix firm that provides part-time CFO services to small businesses, to supply a sample cash flow projection. The chart on page 90 shows ABC Company's operating cash, beginning in January, and outlines its estimated sales and expenses through July. You'll see the benefit of making such a chart when you look at the month of April, which shows a deficit. Assuming this business owner prepared the cash flow projections in January, he or she now has four months to come up with a plan for surviving that projected shortfall.

Before we figure out that plan, let's take a closer look at why a cash crunch might occur in the first place. Not all are predictable, of course. When the economy hit the skids in 2008, many business owners found themselves suddenly worrying about making payroll or paying bills. Aside from the economy, here are other reasons why cash crunches happen:

- A big customer falls behind in payments

- A normally busy season is unexpectedly slow

- Manufacturing, shipping or other business costs rise

- Inventory is mismanaged

- Expansion into new space or territory is overly expensive or poorly timed

ABC COMPANY, LLC

Internal Cash Flow Projections
January to July, 20X1

	January	February
Operating Cash, Beginning	**$125,000**	**$82,000**
Sources of Cash		
Receivable Collections	225,000	200,000
Customer Deposits	10,000	15,000
Loans from the Bank—Revolving Line	-	25,000
Other	-	-
Total Sources of Cash, Including Beginning	360,000	322,000
Uses of Cash		
Payroll, Including Payroll Taxes	65,000	65,000
Accounts Payable—Vendors	45,000	45,000
Other Overhead, Including Rent	60,000	60,000
Owners' Guaranteed Payments	28,000	28,000
Line of Credit Payments	50,000	40,000
Debt Service Payments	25,000	25,000
Capital Expenditures from Operations	-	-
Income Taxes—Prior Year	-	-
Estimated Income Taxes—Current Year	-	-
Other	5,000	5,000
Total Uses of Cash	278,000	268,000
Excess (Deficit) of Cash	**$82,000**	**$54,000**

KEY ASSUMPTIONS:

1. 80% of sales will be collected the month after the sale.

2. 20% of sales will be collected the second month after the sale.

3. Payables are due in thirty days.

4. 75% of eligible receivables can be used for the revolving line of credit.

Source: Jerry L. Mills, CPA, founder and CEO of B2B CFO

Because it's tough to predict the circumstances your business will find itself in weeks or months down the road, it's always smart to have a cash cushion. The next best thing is to have a line of credit (see Chapter 3, page 32) to cover short-term cash shortages, which might happen if there's a lag time in accounts receivables coming in.

	March	April	May	June	July
	$54,000	**$11,000**	**$(58,000)**	**$(11,000)**	**$8,000**
	175,000	225,000	250,000	275,000	250,000
	10,000	12,000	10,000	15,000	10,000
	35,000	55,000	35,000	30,000	20,000
	3,000	–	–	–	–
	277,000	303,000	237,000	309,000	288,000
	70,000	65,000	65,000	70,000	65,000
	38,000	55,000	45,000	55,000	45,000
	60,000	60,000	60,000	60,000	60,000
	28,000	28,000	28,000	28,000	28,000
	30,000	20,000	20,000	20,000	20,000
	25,000	25,000	25,000	25,000	25,000
	10,000	–	–	–	–
	–	65,000	–	–	–
	–	38,000	–	38,000	–
	5,000	5,000	5,000	5,000	5,000
	266,000	361,000	248,000	301,000	248,000
	$11,000	**$(58,000)**	**$(11,000)**	**$8,000**	**$40,000**

> The company is projecting negative cash in April. What can be done in January to make sure the company does not run out of cash in April?

If your company (like the ABC Company) has forecast or found itself in an unexpected cash crunch, there are some ways to fix this cash emergency:

- **Get out there and sell.** Jump-start cash flow by finding new customers or tending to existing ones. Even if your gut is

GETTING CUSTOMERS TO PAY UP

The culprit in your company's cash flow mess may be the foot-dragging client who's not paying the bills.

For most business owners, prodding a customer to pay up is an unpleasant task. That's why it's best to come up with payment policies that you share with accounts ahead of time, to avoid a cash crunch and an awkward strain on your relationship.

Here are some effective strategies:

- Be clear from the get-go about payment terms. The best option is to insist upon full payment up front, either by cash or by credit card. If that's not possible or appropriate, require a deposit, and spread payments out over time according to deadlines. Set a specific date for full payment.

- Make sure payment terms (including late fees) are highlighted in contracts and communicated to customers. Small business owners sometimes rely on verbal agreements, which is a big mistake. Contracts not only are legally binding but also serve as useful tools; a business owner can politely call a customer and point out that, according to the contract, payment is past due and needs immediate attention. If the customer still doesn't pay, follow up with a letter charging late fees.

- Get help. Small business owners often hire accounts receivable clerks to review customer invoices and handle bill collection. If payments are exceptionally late, a company can hire a collections agency, although that's costly and almost certain to impede any future relationship with the customer. As a last resort, a small business can take a deadbeat customer to small claims court.

wrenching, it's critical to make sales calls. Keep in mind that your competitors may be waiting to steal your business—especially if word has gotten out that you're in a bind.

- **Step up collection efforts.** Analyze your receivables. Do your customers owe you money? If so, then it's time to get aggressive about collecting debts. For more on that, see the box "Getting Customers to Pay Up" on page 92. You might also consider giving some customers discounts for early payment, Mills suggests.

- **Review your line of credit.** See if there is room to borrow, or ask your banker to increase the ceiling if you need more money to cover the deficit.

- **Ask suppliers for a favor.** The people who supply your merchandise, equipment or other products or services don't want to lose your business. Especially if you've been a good customer, your suppliers might extend repayment terms or issue a line of credit.

- **Cut costs.** Downsize to a smaller space, or consider moving back home (to your garage or spare bedroom). Sell off excess furniture or office equipment. Trim principals' salaries. Conduct layoffs, as unpleasant as that may be, if it means keeping the business alive.

THE WORST-CASE SCENARIO

My business, in operation for more than eight years, has been slow lately. There is little cash flow and debts are past due. Unsecured credit cards and business lines are up to their limits. Basically, we can't afford to pay our bills. Will I be held personally liable for the debts and liabilities of the company? Will this affect my personal credit? What are the consequences of filing bankruptcy?

These questions that I received from a reader illustrate probably the most painful position that you can find yourself in as a business

VENDOR FINANCING

In the event you're having cash flow problems, it's possible your vendor will work some type of financing arrangement to keep you as a customer. If you haven't already built a relationship with a vendor, check with industry groups, trade associations or even owners of similar businesses to see which vendors offer financing. Make sure to check a vendor's credentials before signing up—and shop around to get the most favorable terms.

GETTING HELP FROM A DEBT TURNAROUND FIRM

After one small business owner bought a small retail business in Forth Worth, Texas, he realized that the previous owner had misrepresented the revenues. Soon he was behind in paying the company's bills. That's when he turned to debt specialist Financial Technologies of Houston for help.

The debt specialist took on the disgruntled creditors so that he could focus his time and energy on rebuilding his business. The specialist was able to negotiate an extended payment schedule with creditors, which allowed him to settle his debts, avoid bankruptcy and ultimately stay afloat. "If you can hold the people off until you can pay them, it allows you to reorganize and get the thing going again," says the business owner, who declined to have his name published for privacy reasons.

The fee that a debt specialist charges can vary, and usually it's worked into that extended payment schedule. Financial Technologies guarantees that its fees and negotiated settlements will cost less than what the small business client owes. Another firm, Corporate Turnaround of Paramus, New Jersey, charges 35 percent of whatever money it saves the small business client by negotiating with creditors.

The business owner says the same creditors he was once indebted to are now willing to work with him again. "Everybody in business knows you go through hard times—they've all been there," he says.

owner: not only has business ground to a halt, but you're deeply in debt, too.

Your first course of action, of course, is to try some of the cash crunch strategies outlined above. If creditors are circling, you may want to consider using the services of a debt turnaround firm. While they charge a fee, turnaround specialists can help get creditors off your back and assist you in liquidating inventory, selling parts of a business (if applicable) and cutting staff.

The alternatives aren't pretty. Can you be held personally liable for debts and liabilities of your company? Most likely yes. Credit card companies, for instance, typically issue cards (even business credit cards) based on the owner's personal credit and require the owner to assume personal liability.

As for bankruptcy, it's painful, messy, expensive—and should only be used when all other options have been exhausted. Consult an attorney familiar with small business bankruptcies to figure out whether this is the best choice for you and which direction to take. In some cases, it might make sense to file separate bankruptcy cases—one for the business and one for yourself as an individual.

The two most commonly used business bankruptcy proceedings are Chapter 7 and Chapter 11. If you've decided to shut your doors forever, you might consider a Chapter 7 filing, in which you turn your business over to a court-appointed trustee, who will then sell the assets and distribute the cash to your creditors.

If you're hopeful that you may survive this downturn, at least enough to have a business left to sell, you might consider seeking Chapter 11 bankruptcy protection. When you file this type of petition, you come up with a reorganization plan (under the direction of a court-appointed trustee) to repay outstanding debts and continue to operate as a business. In most cases, unless you have personal means, you'll need to obtain debtor-in-possession (DIP) financing to keep the business afloat while in bankruptcy court.

In recent years, with credit tight, many struggling businesses have been unable to file for Chapter 11 because they can't obtain DIP financing. In general, it certainly isn't easy to salvage a business through a Chapter 11 filing, and many business owners who try wind up converting to a Chapter 7 liquidation.

PART TWO

THE MECHANICS OF RUNNING A BUSINESS

CHAPTER 10

MANAGEMENT BASICS

O ne of the toughest things about launching a small business is learning to do everything yourself—especially in the early days, when you can't afford staff.

Muriel Siebert, the first woman to own a seat on the New York Stock Exchange and founder of a brokerage that bears her name, once told me: "When you start a company, the only difference between a chairwoman and a charwoman [a cleaning lady] is the letter *i*." In other words, as a start-up entrepreneur, you'll be performing a full range of tasks related to your business—including those completely beneath your skill level as, say, an über-creative fashion designer or an engineering genius. (I recall one bar owner telling me she couldn't remember how many times she'd unclogged the bar's toilet.) This need to be a jack-of-all-trades can be daunting, particularly if you have little or no management experience.

While you may spend mornings mopping the floors, you might spend afternoons meeting with bankers—and you certainly might find yourself outside your comfort zone. If you're a creative type, then you'll also have to get a handle on your company's finances. If you're a numbers person, you'll have to rely on some inner artistry to design your website or marketing materials. If you're an introvert, you'll need to speak up to win clients, financing or even good deals on office space. If you're an extrovert, you'll have to get better at organization, analysis and the nitty-gritty details of running your company.

In order to understand all the various roles you may have to take on as a small business owner, let's take a closer look at a few basic management areas.

General business management.
In Chapter 2, we discussed the importance of creating and maintaining a business plan, which manages your original vision for your company. Your business plan will also help you manage your goals and expectations, and keep you on course for growth. In addition, many business owners develop written policies and procedures, which can help create a company culture, maintain professionalism and provide a sense of order. Especially as you hire employees, you'll want to have these written systems in place so others can learn to operate the business, too; that's critical if you ever want to take a day off or even a vacation. We'll take a closer look at how to develop written policies and procedures later in this chapter.

As a business owner, you'll also want to enhance your skills in a broad range of areas. For instance, you'll need to learn how to market your products and services, which we'll cover in Chapter 13. You'll also want to boost your ability to plan ahead of time for any number of developments, including growth (Chapter 8), the unexpected (see "Managing for the Unexpected" on page 112) and ultimately your exit from the company (Chapter 16).

Money management.
Learning sound financial principles is critical if you want to succeed as an entrepreneur. In Part One, we looked at the sources of funding for your small business, and also the importance of understanding how cash flows in and out of your company. As a business owner, you'll need to keep track of transactions through bookkeeping; learn how to collect money from customers in a timely manner; determine how and when to make capital investments in equipment or new facilities; and

analyze your current financial position so you can avoid problems (such as a lack of money to make payroll) before they balloon out of your control.

Many business owners use accounting software and rely on CPAs for help with money management. How you manage your personal finances may be an indication of how you'll manage finances as business owner. If you're lacking in that area, try beefing up your own money management skills by investing in personal accounting software, taking a financial literary class and learning how to develop a budget.

Resource management.

Resources include everything from human capital—namely, your all-important employees—to physical resources such as inventory, supplies and equipment. We'll cover how to hire the best candidates in Chapter 14, as well as how to make your office a great workplace and avoid employee lawsuits. To effectively manage employees, you'll want to be able to communicate your vision and provide proper training; you'll also want to motivate your employees by making them feel as if they are part of a larger mission. You'll learn how some business owners do this later in this chapter.

In Chapter 12, we'll look at how technology can help when it comes to tracking inventory, managing shipping and distribution, and maintaining client relationships. Managing physical resources also requires financial savvy, as you'll want to negotiate for the best rates and learn how to make use of business-expenses tax deductions.

NEEDED: BETTER MANAGEMENT SKILLS

Are you worried that your skills might be lacking?

First-time entrepreneurs in particular can benefit from the wisdom of someone who's been there and done that and is willing to share lessons learned. That's why I recommend finding a mentor, relying on a trusted professional (such as a lawyer, accountant or strategic advisor) or hiring a coach to help shepherd your company to success, particularly in its initial years. No matter how much experience you have, getting advice from someone who is an industry expert or who understands the process of starting a small business can help prevent missteps along the way.

MENTORS

A mentor is often thought of as a sounding board: someone who can offer feedback, constructive criticism and perhaps a boost of confidence when needed. Mentors are typically seasoned or retired business owners who find it rewarding to help a newbie entrepreneur get out of the gate. It's a good idea to meet with your mentor on an ongoing basis, such as quarterly meetings. If you don't have someone in mind, here are a few opportunities for finding a mentor:

• **The government.** Free counseling is available through the SBA's Small Business Development Centers (www.sba .gov/aboutsba/sbaprograms/sbdc/sbdclocator/SBDC_ LOCATOR.html) and its SCORE affiliate (www.score .org/findscore/index.html), both of which have chapters throughout the country. Counselors can talk to you about writing a business plan, managing cash flow or getting a loan.

• **Industry and trade associations.** There's a group for every specialty, whether that's dry cleaning (Drycleaning and Laundry Institute), bouquet making (Society of American Florists) or financial planning (Financial Planning Association). By attending meetings, conferences or networking events, you can meet a mentor who can give you industry-specific advice, such as what might be the best pricing structure for your business.

• **Business groups and alumni networks.** A number of professional associations offer support to members, whether that's the Entrepreneurs' Organization, the National Association of Women Business Owners or the Hispanic Chamber of Commerce. Your alma mater may be helpful, especially if you attended a business school.

Professional Advisors or Consultants

Two professionals will doubtlessly serve you well in managing your business: an accountant and a lawyer. An accountant can help you with tax forms, business planning and general advice on everything from leasing versus buying to setting up a retirement plan. A lawyer can help you set up your company's legal structure, protect you from liability and advise you on state or federal rules when it comes to, say, hiring employees. Consider your needs when selecting both, and make sure to ask other business owners for references. Ask up front about rates (in particular, ask if they bill for basic phone calls or e-mails). Consultants in other fields can help you design your website, launch an online advertising campaign or set up an IT system, among other things. Again, references from other business owners can help you find the professional services you need.

Coaches

A coach can help you improve management skills, often by getting you to think more like a CEO and less like a worker bee. Many business owners seek out a coach (sometimes called a life coach, and other times a business, career or executive coach) when they have become overworked, overwhelmed and generally frazzled. A coach—much as in sports—is supposed to help you perform at peak levels. The field is relatively new, and professional standards are just emerging. The International Coach Federation, the Association of Career Professionals and Coach U provide directories of coaches. We'll take a look in the next section at how one business owner used a coach to improve his management skills.

MANAGE YOURSELF FIRST

In the start-up years, the necessity of dictating how everything around you is done can serve you well. Hyperattention to detail, intimate knowledge of your company's operations and the lessons you learn by doing it all yourself are invaluable.

Unfortunately, many business owners become control freaks. When the business finally grows enough to hire staff, these control-freak business owners aren't willing to let workers do their jobs. Instead, they watch over employees' shoulders, trying to make sure everything is done exactly the way they would do it themselves. They become maddening, arrogant and overbearing, and they pretty much refuse to leave the building. And they're generally miserable.

What's important to remember is that while you must be hands-on in the early days of running a company, you also must step back to allow it to grow. (See Chapter 8 for more on growing your business.)

For instance, Robert Smith, owner of Champion Media Worldwide, a search engine marketing firm in Rockton, Illinois, learned this lesson the hard way. Smith recalls doing everything when he was starting up: meeting with clients, handling all the bills, writing marketing materials, even running to the copy shop as needed. "I had to be a control freak, because I had to do everything," he says.

Smith worked twelve-hour days, spent time away from his family and never took vacations. He began hiring employees in 2004, but that didn't help matters much, as he didn't trust anyone to do things as well as he could. Fed up, he finally turned to a business coach and got some advice that opened his eyes: until he released some control, the business would never take off.

Entrepreneurs are "notorious for having blind spots," Smith says. "We get into a way of doing things. Sometimes, it takes someone from the outside to look at your business model and strategies and help you tune it up."

Taking tips from his business coach, Smith began training his eleven employees on a new system that could run without him (one step he's taken is to write out his company's policies and procedures). "With me not having to do everything and being able to delegate, that allowed me to concentrate on bigger and better deals," he says. "I'm not the guy making copies— I can focus on stuff that brings in the business." While he still fights the urge to micromanage, he can't argue with the results. Smith's new approach has added more than $100,000 to the company's coffers, and he finally took a real vacation— to the Wisconsin Dells, a Midwest tourist destination—for the first time in ten years. "Now," he says, "I feel like I have a real business."

DEVELOPING WRITTEN POLICIES AND PROCEDURES

Every business, no matter how small, needs to have standards, and developing your own set of policies and procedures (often called an operations manual) will help your business run more smoothly—especially when you can't be there. In the event you were to become ill or incapacitated, the manual would help someone else—whether that's your business partner, your employees or even a family member—run the company until you're back in action.

It's also important to have a written system in place when you begin to hire employees, as you'll want others to understand every detail of how *you* want the business run. (An operations manual shouldn't be confused with an employee handbook, which focuses more on workplace rules and can help protect you in the event of a lawsuit. See Chapter 14.) For instance, how do you like customers greeted when they come in the door? Or what day of the month do you order supplies from a vendor? Where do you keep the extra set of keys to the storage room?

Every operations manual is different, so there's no exact formula to follow. You'll want to create one that essentially maps out exactly how things get done in your specific business. Start with your company's mission statement, the products and services it offers, and any goals or values about your business that you may wish to communicate to others. (See the box "Setting a Standard of Excellence" on page 108.) Include an organizational chart and job descriptions. After that, you may want to break instructions down into distinct areas, including:

- How-to procedures, such as how to open and close your office, store, warehouse or other physical locations

- Phone numbers, e-mail addresses and other ways to reach clients, vendors, suppliers, insurance companies, the security company and other important contacts

- Business-related policies, such as whether you issue refunds or accept payment by credit card (for emergency procedures, see "Managing for the Unexpected" on page 112).

The operations manual, essentially, is a tool kit for replicating your knowledge of your business and what you do on any given day. As your business grows, you may wish to have separate manuals for different departments or divisions. You might also develop a basic version for entry-level employees and a more detailed version (with sensitive information on finances, for example) for senior managers.

David Wong, a dentist in Tulsa, Oklahoma, built his practice from the ground up, and now has a thriving business worth more than $1 million. Wong, who also serves as a business coach to dentists, says he was able to train his employees—and empower them to run the operation if need be—by writing out all his policies and procedures. Wong found it easiest to break his business down into five categories—organization, marketing/sales, people, technology and capital—and advises other entrepreneurs to come up with categories that make sense for their businesses. "Think up everything you do on a daily basis, and try to put them into one of these categories," he says. Keep in mind that some parts of your operations manual, such as those pertaining to employee hiring/firing and financial matters, should be confidential or accessible only by high-level managers. Here's how he tells other business owners to write an operations manual, based on how he did it:

Organization.

Write out all that's involved in your daily operations. Outline who's in charge of opening the business for the day and exactly how they should go about doing that. Provide specific instructions: park in the back, enter through the side entrance, unlock the door, disarm the security system, turn on all the lights, unlock all the doors and change the sign to Open. You'll also want to write down how to answer the phone, how to greet a customer, how to handle an angry client and any other related matters.

Marketing/sales.

You'll want to keep track of basic information, such as where your business cards, brochures, direct mail pieces and other promotional materials are printed, and how often. You'll want to describe how leads are generated, how they are followed up, how your company handles customer service, and anything else that has to do with generating new and repeat business.

People.

You'll want to write down all your staff positions, plus the job descriptions. For your current staff, record details of when (and how) each employee began or ended employment. Include a copy of your employee handbook, which covers everything from how employees should dress to how they earn bonuses and vacations.

SETTING A STANDARD OF EXCELLENCE

When Joe Albanese, a captain in the Navy Reserve, started his Newton, Massachusetts, construction management company in 2005, he knew in the back of his mind that he might be called back into service. Three years later, it happened. In February 2008, Albanese was sent to the Middle East, where he served for seven months. But before he deployed, Albanese decided to write down the "Six Qualities of Excellence" he wanted his managers and employees to possess in his absence: the confidence to take charge, the capacity to anticipate, the ability to focus on details, the spirit to collaborate, the creativity to innovate and the knowledge to problem-solve. Albanese came up with the qualities after an off-site brainstorming meeting with eight members of his executive team. To communicate those values to the rest of the ninety-six-person staff, he held an all-company meeting to launch the "Six Qualities of Excellence" and posted them on the company's website. But he didn't stop there. "We printed the qualities on the back of our business cards and corporate note cards," he says. "We hung Plexiglas posters in our lobby. We even named our conference rooms after the six qualities."

In his absence, Albanese's company, Commodore Builders, never skipped a beat, growing 40 percent to nearly $80 million in revenues—a performance that Albanese credits to employees' understanding not just their day-to-day jobs but also his mission and vision for the business.

Technology.

Outline all the machines, computers, software and equipment that you use to keep your business up and running. Discuss how your various pieces of technology operate, what they do, how they are maintained, who needs to use them and how employees are trained to use them.

Capital.

Include your company's financial statements and an explanation of how your budget is made and evaluated. Cover numerous details related to your company's financing operations, such as whether you have or are seeking loans, what to do with profits, how you set fees or prices for your goods or services, how you handle payroll and any details of your lease, if applicable.

Wong admits that it took some time to write out his company's policies and procedures into an operations manual, which he updates as needed. But now, especially as he views the different categories, "it is easier to see the big picture of operating a business," he says. "The task is not so daunting. It can even be kind of fun!"

MANAGING YOUR EMPLOYEES

Motivating, supervising and managing people is an essential part of running a business. If you've never managed employees before, there are plenty of resources available to you, including mentors, coaches and fellow business owners. The SBA also offers a primer on its site, at www.sba.gov/smallbusiness planner/manage/manageemployees/index.html.

The best way to manage staff is to make sure you hire the best employees in the first place, which is why I've devoted Chapter 14 to that subject. Nancy Clark, a business consultant in Danville, California, says it's important to identify exactly what you need when hiring for a specific position, and then find the person who can best bring those skills to the job. "The mistake that many if not most leaders make is focusing exclusively on a person's knowledge, experience and training," she says. "We must also focus on a candidate's work style or behavioral profile—do they have the natural strengths to do the job?" One way to figure that out is to invite a candidate in for a tryout (see page 149). If a person is lacking in those natural strengths, then don't place him or her in the position. "It will only result in failure for both the business and the employee," she says.

As you start to hire people, you'll see why it was so important to develop a mission statement back when you were starting your company. That's the first tool you can use to communicate to staff exactly what you and your company are all about. You can't expect employees to live up to your expectations if you don't clearly define what they are. Providing employees with clear instructions on how to perform a job (which you should outline in your operations manual) and an employee handbook will go a long way in avoiding confusion, tension or bad performance. Meeting regularly with staff, answering their questions and asking for their opinions also will win their trust and loyalty.

When problems arise, it's important to determine the cause. "It may be the supervisor, it may be unclear responsibilities, it may be a mismatch of the job to employee," says Clark. "By getting to the root of the problem, an astute manager can address the issue appropriately." You may need to meet privately with the employee, make some adjustments and then clearly lay out your expectations again. Give employees a chance to improve, and consider letting them go if they continue to fail to meet those expectations. (See "When It's Not Working Out" on page 154.)

If employees are dealing with personal situations—whether coping with a legal issue or finding an elder care facility for an ailing parent—you may want to provide them with a small chunk of time off (with pay). If they need more time off, offer them unpaid leave. Keep in mind that businesses with more than fifty employees are required to comply with the Family and Medical Leave Act, which provides employees with up to twelve weeks of unpaid, job-protected leave a year to care for a new baby, an ill family member or their own serious health condition. See if other staff can help in their coworker's absence. You may also want to allow for flexible scheduling, permitting an employee to adjust starting and quitting times, work from home or even share a job with other employees.

To motivate employees, ask workers to step away from their

routine jobs on occasion and take on a special project, such as coming up with a creative solution to a customer's problem. The goal is to make your staff feel important and that they're not just punching the clock. "The single best way to motivate employees is to make them feel like they are part of the success of the company," says Angela Jia Kim, founder of Om Aroma, an organic skin care line, and Savor the Success, a women's public relations cooperative. "Everyone has a talent that can help build business. The boss's job is to identify this talent and cultivate it. When people use their talents, there is more flow at work, and employees assume more responsibility. This is key to managing."

Some companies, like Tasty Catering in Chicago, practice open-book management, in which relevant financial information is shared with all employees so that they better understand the company's performance. Each week, a six-page internal newsletter is sent via e-mail to every staff member, showing the current period's sales compared to a year earlier, says owner Tom Walter. "These communication methods stimulate motivation," he says. Many companies provide performance-based rewards to staff, especially those who sell a company's products or services. Rewards often come in the form of cash (or equity in the company) but can be noncash items such as gift cards, merchandise or travel packages. A 2009 survey by Deloitte Consulting found that companies, in a bid to control costs and get a better return on investment, are increasingly setting performance goals as they redesign compensation plans.

You'll also want to have fun with your staff, to develop good morale. Trucking company Admiral Merchants Motor Freight in Minneapolis, which has about sixty employees, encourages its office staff to exercise through an original program called "Run to the Border." Staff who agree to work out for thirty minutes a day, five days a week, for an entire year periodically get gift certificates to restaurants and the local sporting goods store. (A year's worth of workouts equates to 1,500 miles, roughly the distance between their office and the Mexican border.) April Williams, owner of North Star Marketing in North Kingstown, Rhode Island, also uses fitness as a morale booster, paying a trainer to come in one morning a week to lead hourlong workout sessions in her company's conference room. Usually, about half of her ten-member staff takes part, and the fitness sessions help with team building and boost employee loyalty, she says.

If an exercise routine doesn't work for your staff, consider something like an NCAA basketball tournament or an Oscars pool, and hand out awards to the winners. You might host a holiday or end-of-fiscal-year party to thank staff for their hard work. At Total Attorneys in Chicago, a managed-services provider to the legal industry, owner Ed Scanlan gives away sports, theater and concert tickets, and encourages his 170 employees to become "friends" on Facebook, the social networking site, to foster a feeling of camaraderie. "The more friendships people develop within the workplace, the more likely they are to stay with the company," he says.

MANAGING FOR THE UNEXPECTED

No matter how good you are as a businessperson and manager, there will always be circumstances beyond your control that can affect your business. Remember Greg Mangiaracina in Chapter 1, whose home inspection business was displaced by Hurricane Katrina?

No one likes to think about such large-scale catastrophes as devastating hurricanes, earthquakes or—in today's world—terrorist attacks. Fortunately, those events are rare, but smaller "disasters," such as computer crashes and power outages, can wreak havoc on a small firm.

Preparing for the worst can help minimize the risk. Sample disaster plans are widely available on the Internet, including the SBA's website, and can be customized for your business needs.

Here's a short list of how to prepare to best protect your business, should disaster strike:

- **Review insurance policies.** It's smart for any business owner to take out property insurance policies, which cover the cost of replacing damaged or destroyed equipment or buildings. But also consider business interruption insurance, which covers lost income in the event that your business is forced to shut down temporarily.

- **Develop a contingency plan.** Come up with a list of backup vendors or suppliers in case your primary ones are shut down. Consider alternative work sites so that you can keep operating. Keep a list of twenty four-hour emergency numbers for all your employees, and develop a quick and efficient way of keeping employees informed.

- **Back it up.** Make backup copies of all critical records, such as accounting and employee data, customer lists, production formulas and inventory. Keep that information in a separate location at least fifty miles away, or subscribe to a online data backup service provider.

CHAPTER 11

LEGAL STRUCTURES

Whether you're starting a business from home or opening a large-scale operation, you'll need to decide on the best legal structure for your new company. Don't underestimate the importance of your choice, as the legal entity you choose will affect how much personal liability you face, how much you pay in taxes and how in-depth your new company's record keeping will need to be.

Your business structure can take one of five basic forms: the sole proprietorship, the partnership, the regular or C corporation, the S corporation, and the increasingly popular limited liability company or LLC. The best entity for you will depend on the type of business you'll run, your potential exposure to lawsuits, the number of owners and whether you want the ability to raise capital or transfer shares. It's smart, and in many cases necessary, to consult a lawyer or accountant when making your choice. You may also take advantage of a number of resources available on the Internet, including LegalZoom.com and Nolo.com, which offer legal forms and do-it-yourself kits at reasonable prices.

We'll delve into more details on each of the five structures in the coming pages, but first let's take a brief look at how the needs of a select group of business owners guided their decisions. A few years back, Kevin Caron, then a truck driver in Phoenix, started doing artwork on the side, creating bells, fountains and outdoor sculptures from unusual materials. In 2006, he quit trucking, opened up his own art studio and quickly won more than thirty public, private and commercial commissions. As his business grew, he decided to seek liability protection. Caron set up an LLC, based on his attorney's recommendation, and enjoys its easy bookkeeping compared to that of a regular corporation.

In Springfield, Illinois, Mary Byers, a professional speaker and author, wanted liability protection but wasn't sure if an S corporation or an LLC would be best. She quizzed other entrepreneurs on which structures they chose, read several books on incorporating and consulted an attorney and two accountants. She eventually settled on an S corporation, chiefly to save on self-employment taxes—and because the LLC didn't seem to provide as many benefits in Illinois as it does in other states.

And in New York, entrepreneur Landy Ung knew for sure that the best structure for her start-up company, 8coupons.com, was the C corporation. Ung is hoping to attract investors to her company, which sends coupons to users' cell phones. She's been advised by venture capitalists that using a C corporations allows 8coupons.com to be a stand-alone entity (free of personal or shareholder liability) with transferable shares.

While you should consider your long-term needs, keep in mind that your choice of entity doesn't have to be permanent. You might launch a home-based business as a sole proprietorship, for instance, but convert to an LLC or corporation when you move into new space, hire employees or become more vulnerable to lawsuits.

Here's a look at each of the different structures.

SOLE PROPRIETORSHIPS

The vast majority of small businesses start off as sole proprietorships, which are the simplest and least expensive vehicles to create and operate, according to the SBA. With a sole proprietorship, the owner and the business are essentially one and the same, meaning you have complete control, you can make decisions as you see fit and the profits from the business flow through to your personal tax return as Schedule C income. (If you don't have profits, you may be entitled to a business loss that can help offset other income.) To launch a sole proprietorship, you don't need to file legal forms or paperwork, such as articles of incorporation, but you might have to obtain a business license, depending on state law. (See the box "Do I Need a Business License or Permit?" on page 118.) A sole proprietorship can only be used by an individual who owns the company, unless it's a husband-and-wife team, in which case it can be shared.

The main drawback of setting up a sole proprietorship is that you have unlimited personal responsibility for all debts or judgments related to the business. That liability, in turn, may make it difficult to attract investors or raise funds for your business.

As a sole proprietor, you'll also be responsible for paying the full burden of Social Security and Medicare taxes—a cost normally split between employer and employee. For 2009, the first $106,800 of self-employment income was taxed at 12.4 percent for Social Security and 2.9 percent for Medicare. Any amount over $106,800 continues to be taxed at 2.9 percent for Medicare only. For current rates, visit Social Security online at www.ssa.gov.

PARTNERSHIPS

When two or more people (not spouses) start a business together, a sole proprietorship isn't an option. Instead, the owners may form a general partnership, which is much like the sole proprietorship in that it can be established easily and requires minimal cost or paperwork (some states might require a basic partnership certificate stating the partners' names, aside from other business licenses). The profits from a partnership

DO I NEED A BUSINESS LICENSE OR PERMIT?

Before launching your business, make sure you have all the necessary paperwork. Here's a list of some of the various licenses and permits you may be required to file:

Local licenses, permits and registrations

Most states and many cities or counties require that you obtain a license, permit or registration when you start a business, typically for tax purposes and sometimes to protect public health and safety.

To obtain: Check your state's website for information on how to comply with your particular state's requirements; also check county and city websites.

Professional licenses

Certain occupations and professions—running the gamut from self-employed doctors and hairdressers to contractors and funeral home directors—require special licensing.

To obtain: Consult with your occupation's governing agency, be it a state bar association, medical board or health department's cosmetology board, for the particular requirements in your locality.

Employer Identification Number or charter

On the federal level, if you're a sole proprietor with employees, or a partnership, LLC or corporation, you'll need to obtain an Employer Identification Number, a unique nine-digit number that's often considered a corporate equivalent to a Social Security number. Sole proprietors without employees technically don't need EINs because they can use their Social Security numbers on any business-related forms. Some sole proprietors, however, prefer using an EIN to keep business and personal affairs separate, and to guard against identity theft.

To obtain: It's easy (and free) to obtain an EIN from the Internal Revenue Service's website. For more on obtaining an EIN, visit www.irs.gov and search on "EIN."

If your business is headquartered in a state that collects income tax, you'll also need to obtain a state employer identification number or charter.

To obtain: Check with your state's treasury department or department of revenue.

State tax license

If you're engaged in the sale of goods or services, you'll likely need to obtain a state tax license. The rules vary by state, but generally most things sold to customers are taxable—with major exceptions such as food and prescription drugs—and the government simply finds it easier to make the seller (that's you) collect sales tax. You'll get it from your customer and then eventually send it along to the state.

To obtain: Check with you state's sales tax authority (typically the Department of Revenue). For a helpful list, try the Sales Tax Clearinghouse, www.thestc.com, and click on "State Tax Rates and DoR Webpages."

State labor department registration

If you have employees, you'll likely need to register with your state's labor department or any other agency that administers unemployment insurance contributions and workers' compensation. Rules vary by state; some states may require you to buy workers' compensation insurance from a state agency rather than your insurance carrier.

To obtain: Check with your state's labor department. Some states might also have special websites with information geared toward small business labor issues; for instance, in New York try www.nylovessmallbiz.com/starting/employer.htm, or in Oregon try www.oregon.gov/DCBS/SBO/index.shtml.

flow through to the partners' personal income tax returns. Partners may split profits equally, or decide one or more partners deserve a greater share for contributing either more assets or work hours to the business. Each partner then pays self-employment taxes on his or her share.

Also like a sole proprietorship, a general partnership doesn't protect against personal liability—and in addition, partners are held responsible for the actions of the other partners. But perhaps the greatest risk with a partnership is the possibility of disagreement and, along with that, disappointment and frustration that can threaten the livelihood of the business. When two or more people start a company together, it's wise (but not legally required) for them to craft a written, carefully thought-out partnership agreement. Much like a prenuptial agreement, the partnership agreement spells out who brings what to the relationship, such as cash or property, and outlines what happens if either partner wants out, dies, becomes disabled or stops performing. Options such as a buyout or sale of the partner's interest should be included in a buy-sell clause or, if complex, in a separate agreement.

Many partners, especially those starting retail or service businesses, will choose to establish a general partnership, although they might also consider forming an LLC or corporation to protect liability, receive different tax treatment or other reasons. In addition, two other but less common partnerships are outlined below.

LIMITED PARTNERSHIP

A more formal and complex arrangement than a general partnership, the limited partnership has one or more general partners who make management decisions and one or more limited partners who are passive investors. While the general partners are personally liable for the debts of the venture, the limited partners are liable only to the extent of their investment. An LP may be appropriate for a small but growing business that wants to raise money by selling limited partnership interests in the company.

LIMITED LIABILITY PARTNERSHIP

With this vehicle, partners are liable for the company's business debts and for their own negligence, but not the negligence of other partners. The LLP is commonly used by doctors, lawyers and other professionals who want to establish a practice together.

C CORPORATION

The regular or C corporation is considered a legal entity that's completely separate from the owner or owners who create and manage its operations. The most common reason for setting one up is to protect your personal assets (such as your home, investments or retirement accounts) from any business-related liabilities; if the corporation goes belly-up, owners (called shareholders) lose their investment but won't be held liable for any debt owed to the company's creditors. Also, each owner is responsible for his or her own personal negligence or misdeeds but not that of co-owners.

Corporations issue stock and are run by a board of directors (or, in smaller companies, a single director) who oversee major decisions and operating procedures. The issuance of stock makes it easier to attract investors and high-caliber employees, who may be motivated by the chance to own a piece of the company.

A drawback to forming a C corporation is the so-called double taxation of corporate profits. Because it's a separate entity, the corporation pays taxes at the corporate rate on all income that's left after business expenses (including salaries) are paid. That income is taxed again when it's distributed as dividends to owners (shareholders) at their own individual income tax rate. To avoid double taxation, some owners prefer to set up an S corporation (see below). The C corporation does provide some tax advantages, however. For instance, if you want to keep profits within the company for growth or expansion, rather than paying them out, the money may be taxed at a lower corporate rate than what you would pay as an individual.

Corporations take time and money to set up, and it's best to consult a lawyer familiar with the formalities of creating and maintaining such an entity. You'll need to pay a filing fee (which varies by state) and prepare a document called the articles of incorporation. Check the website of your state's secretary of state for a fill-in-the-blank form. Generally, you need to adopt bylaws, appoint officers and directors and hold annual meetings, although many states allow smaller corporations to operate in a less formal manner.

S CORPORATION

Some business owners prefer to set up an S corporation, which provides liability protection while allowing profits to pass through to the owners' personal tax returns. This special tax status (its letter refers to subchapter S of the Internal Revenue Code) prevents the double taxation scenario created under a C corporation.

Owners of S corporations can reduce their overall tax bill by paying themselves a salary, subject to payroll taxes (Social Security and Medicare taxes), and then taking a dividend, which is distributed free of employment taxes (and, again, isn't subject to the corporate tax rate). There's a catch, though: that salary must be reasonable, which can be determined by researching salaries in similar industries in the same geographic region. The IRS is well aware that many owners of S corporations are tempted to underreport salary to avoid paying payroll taxes, while taking a hefty payroll-tax-free dividend. To avoid trouble with the IRS, set your salary at a reasonable level based on salaries for comparable positions—and keep careful records in the event of an IRS audit.

To set up an S corporation, you follow the same steps for setting up a regular corporation but take the extra step of electing S status via a special IRS form. To qualify for S corporation status, you must meet certain rules, such as having fewer than one hundred shareholders and issuing only one class of stock (preferred shares aren't allowed).

LIMITED LIABILITY COMPANY

The limited liability company, or LLC, is a relatively new entity that has become a popular choice among small business owners because it offers liability protection, flexibility and tax efficiency, according to Alan C. Ederer, a partner at Westerman Ball Ederer Miller & Sharfstein, LLP, in Mineola, New York, who advises his business-owner clients on the LLC. With an LLC, your liability is generally limited to how much you put into the company, so you're not responsible for the company's debt beyond your personal investment, with the exception of any business debt you personally guarantee, such as a business loan or line of credit, or any misdeeds that you personally commit, for which you are also on the hook. The management structure of an LLC is less formal than that of a corporation, so owners can freely divvy up operational duties and don't need to keep minutes, pass resolutions or hold annual meetings. More important, the structure allows for the same pass-through taxation of sole proprietorships, partnerships and S corporations. That means owners avoid the C corporation's double tax trap.

Of course, forming an LLC is not quite as easy as a sole proprietorship or partnership. You'll need to prepare articles of organization, which are generally filed with your state's secretary of state. Some states provide fill-in-the-black forms, requesting standard information such as the LLC's name, business purpose and type of management (such as member-managed, where all owners take part in management, or manager-managed, where some owners manage while others act as passive investors). Some states may ask for an operating agreement, which, much like a partnership agreement, outlines each owner's responsibilities, his or her share of profits or losses, and what happens if any owner wants out. Even if your state doesn't legally require one, it's wise to have an operating agreement to avoid or resolve any problems that may arise. For more on what your state requires of an LLC, visit the website of your state's secretary of state.

An LLC can also be suitable for the single owner who wants the liability coverage of a corporation but the more simplified tax treatment and operational freedom of a sole proprietorship. The LLC is often described as a hybrid vehicle that maximizes the advantages of other structures while minimizing the disadvantages.

The SBA's website further outlines the forms of ownership and basic structures, providing a helpful resource as you decide which is the best fit for your business. Visit the choose-a-structure feature at www.sba.gov/smallbusinessplanner/start/chooseastructure/index.html. In addition, the IRS's site outlines the income tax forms you'll need to file based on your business structure. Visit the IRS's site at www.irs.gov/businesses/small/article/0,,id=98359,00.html.

Before proceeding to create any type of business structure, I recommend that you consult with your attorney and other relevant professionals, such as your tax advisor or accountant. There are complex legal and tax issues involved, and you'll want to make sure you've made the wisest choice for your new business.

CHAPTER 12

TECHNOLOGY

Technological advances have greatly increased the ease with which you can run and grow a small business. If only technology weren't so complicated.

These days, it's tough for any entrepreneur to make it—let alone succeed—without a heavy dose of tech. You need a well-designed and easy-to-use website (that's a no-brainer), plus you might benefit greatly from software, Web applications and equipment that allow you to mange inventory, track customers' purchases, process invoices, manage payroll and communicate with staff. Most entrepreneurs want the freedom to leave the office yet still stay connected, meaning they (and key staff) need to be outfitted with cell phones, laptops and wireless devices.

Not long ago, the latest technology was only available to the biggest companies with the deepest pockets. Now, prices have dropped as big players such as Microsoft, Oracle, IBM and SAP try to tap the small business market. Increasingly, software is becoming available via the Web as "software as a service" or SaaS, replacing more expensive boxed software that needs to be purchased outright and installed. Open-source software, that is, software whose source code is freely available on the Internet for anyone to use or modify, has made it possible for small business owners (usually with the help of developers or consultants) to customize software for their unique needs.

TECHNOLOGY BASICS

If you're just starting out, it's quite possible that you're feeling overwhelmed by the amount of technology you'll need to run your business efficiently and professionally. I asked Ramon Ray, editor of SmallBizTechnology.com, to offer some pointers. He says every small business needs the basics:

- Hardware, such as desktop computers, laptops, phones and wireless devices

- Software, from a simple word processing program to industry-specific applications

- A server, which is a central computer that shares data, files and applications and allows you and your employees to access the Internet or use the same printer

- Networking devices, such as routers, hubs and switches, that tie workstations together and provide security features, such as firewalls

Unless you've got a solid background in technology, a computer consultant can be your best friend, Ramon says. To find one, ask other business owners for references, or check with your industry group or trade association for a recommendation. Some consultants, many of whom are small business owners themselves, charge by the hour or the day; others charge a flat rate. When you hire a consultant to install software or build a network, keep in mind you'll probably want help down the road, when the system inevitably crashes or simply needs maintenance. See if you can negotiate a long-term support arrangement as part of your consultant agreement.

Aside from the basics outlined above, you'll also want specific technology products to help your business run more smoothly. What you need may vary by industry. For instance, if your business is paper-intensive—say, it's a law firm or an accounting practice—you may want to invest in a document-imaging system, which allows you to convert paper into electronic files. If you're a retailer, you'll probably need a point-of-sale system, which is essentially an electronic cash register that allows you to track sales. Almost all businesses will benefit from a database program, which allows you to collect, store and organize data, such as contact information for your customers, suppliers and vendors. Before making an investment in a specific product, consider feedback from current users by checking reviews on places like www.cnet.com, www.zdnet.com and www.pcmag.com.

Still overwhelmed? Ray says it's helpful to break your business down into distinct functions and then decide what software or hardware (or combination of both) can help in each area. Here are four common functions:

Sales and Marketing

A host of programs can help you cultivate relationships with clients. More companies are trying customer relationship management or CRM software, which organizes contact information for current and prospective customers, and allows multiple users (such as an entire sales team) to track customers' buying habits. Popular programs include Saleforce.com's SaaS CRM, Microsoft's Dynamics CRM, Maximizer, ACT and Gold-Mine contact manager systems. If you want to promote your business via electronic newsletters, special e-mail marketing software made by Lyris, Oracle, Unica and other providers can help you develop targeted, spam-free e-mails to send to your distribution lists.

Inventory Management and Operations

If you stock merchandise, then bar codes, radiofrequency ID tags, scanners and related software can help you keep track of inventory and fill customers' orders in a more timely fashion. Some businesses use an enterprise resource planning (ERP) system, which pulls from both hardware and software programs to integrate various functions, such as distribution, shipping and invoicing. An ERP system can help a business owner figure out the amount of inventory needed to prevent overstocking, which can reduce overhead. Major players in the ERP space include Microsoft, NetSuite and Aplicor.

Finance and Accounting

Especially if you're not a number cruncher by nature, an accounting software program can help you organize your business finances, track outstanding invoices and figure out how much cash your company has available. Online bookkeeping that keeps track of business expenses will also make life easier (for you and your accountant) during tax season. Many business owners use QuickBooks, MYOB, Peachtree or Microsoft Office.

General Management

A business owner might invest in sophisticated technology called business intelligence software, which culls data from various areas—such as accounting, inventory management and sales—and delivers reports and analysis. BI technology can help an entrepreneur figure out what's driving profits and pinpoint areas in the company that aren't running smoothly. IBM Congos, Sage, SAP, MicroStrategy and SAS Institute offer BI tools.

BUILDING YOUR WEBSITE

Customers expect most small businesses to maintain dynamic websites, where a company's services and location are listed and, if appropriate, where products or services can easily be

SHOULD I INVEST IN MACS OR PCS?

These days, the answer really depends on the software you plan to use. Not long ago, personal computers running Microsoft Windows were the industry standard; now, Macintosh computers, which have won the hearts of many consumers, are being seen as a solution for small to medium businesses.

The software, however, is another story. A number of applications—chief among them Intuit's popular QuickBooks accounting software—were designed for PCs. Versions for Macs either don't operate as well or simply don't exist; because Mac claims only a small piece of the computer market, some software developers don't create versions for Apple lovers.

That said, many business owners enjoy Mac's ease of use and prefer a system that they'll need to fix, support and worry about a lot less than PCs. Hackers, much like legitimate software developers, concentrate their efforts on other operating systems, so big virus threats to Mac users are rare. Macs are also popular for business owners who do design work.

There's no clear-cut winner, as both Macs and PCs bring advantages to the table. Consider your top needs, and if you're not tech-savvy, ask a computer expert (such as a consultant who can help you develop a system) before making your purchase. Some companies might want both to fully cover their needs.

purchased with the click of a mouse. More people, in general, are making purchases online: in 2007, online retail sales hit $175 billion, a 21 percent increase over $144.6 billion in 2006, according to Forrester Research.

With that in mind, the technological priority for any business—whether you have a bricks-and-mortar sporting goods store that needs another sales outlet or a dental practice that needs to list services, office location and practitioner bios online—should be the development of a website. If you don't already have one (and many entrepreneurs are slow to get a dazzling website up and running), it's not too late to get started. Here's a guide to the essential components when it comes to taking your business online:

PICK A DOMAIN NAME

Chances are your dream URL is already taken. Domain-name registries—companies such as VeriSign, Go Daddy Group, Moniker.com and Register.com—say don't waste your time trying to come up with a catchy five-letter name that ends in .com. Every last one is gone, as are three- and four-letter configurations. What to do? You can opt for a less popular extension (think .net, .info or .biz). You can also attempt to buy a previously registered domain name on an aftermarket auction site, such as GoDaddy's TDNAM.com. Or you can come up with a memorable but more unusual name or phrase, a strategy that worked for Jason Levin. Levin, the founder of Gringos Ventures, a contract flower grower in Vista, California wanted to start an online floral shop, so he decided to purchase the name SunflowerGuy.com for $2,500 in the aftermarket. (He says it was worth it, though he might have reconsidered the name if the price had been any higher.) One caveat to this approach: make sure your name or phrase isn't too unusual, unless you have a hefty marketing budget.

FIND THE PERFECT HOST

Next, you'll need to find a company that will host, or provide room on its servers for your company's website. Major players such as Verizon Online, Yahoo and Lycos and a growing number of boutique firms offer Web-hosting services, sometimes throwing in incentives such as online marketing and Web publishing tools. Make sure to do some comparison shopping, as Web-hosting packages can vary widely in terms of price and services offered. (For instance, some companies offer e-commerce capabilities, while others do not.) Figure out what you need in terms of disk space and bandwidth, particularly if you plan to sell products online. Can't figure out which host to choose? Check message boards to see what other business owners are saying about their Web hosts.

DESIGN YOUR SITE

Your Web-hosting company may offer do-it-yourself templates, or you may hire a Web designer to create the look and features you want. You might also try Web design tools, including Microsoft Expression or Adobe Dreamweaver. Think about the graphics, colors and fonts you want; if you're not sure, visit other websites and find ones that appeal to you. Most experts say keep it simple: nothing blinking, flashing or slow to load. You'll want well-written content, sharp pictures and incentives for people to buy. Consider the navigability of the site—how should pages link? Make sure to include contact information, an "About Us" page and staff bios to give yourself credibility. Once the site is up and running, you'll need to be able to update that content to keep it fresh (too many business owners fail to do so, driving away potential customers with static or—even worse—dated sites). Increasingly, business owners are adding blogs to their sites, or creating profiles on social networking sites to connect with customers. For more on whether this is time well spent for your particular venture, see Chapter 13.

MARKETING

Marketing is all about boosting your company's image, getting your message out there and letting potential customers know about the valuable products and services that your company offers.

How you go about marketing your company depends largely on your budget, your industry, your geographic region of the country and, more important, the type of customer you want to attract.

Technology has drastically transformed marketing strategies in the past decade. Many businesses that once would have taken out an ad in the yellow pages or paid a small sum for a radio or television spot have turned to online vehicles—everything from websites to social networking sites—to make their presence known. Entrepreneurs who once would have tried direct-mail campaigns or gone door-to-door are now turning to e-mail blasts, hoping newsletters with informative content and sales announcements will end up in customers' in-boxes rather than their spam folders.

Still, while the delivery methods may have changed for many businesses, the basic principles of marketing have not. (See the box "Marketing Essentials" on page 134.) Companies can still benefit from the staples: a catchy name, a well-designed logo, custom business cards and letterhead. Business owners with greater budgets for marketing may tap the services of advertising, marketing or branding agencies for help with

MARKETING ESSENTIALS

Need a crash course on marketing? John Jantsch, a marketing and digital technology coach and author of *Duct Tape Marketing,* offers these five tips:

- Marketing is all about reaching your potential customers and making sure they know, like and trust you.

- When coming up with a marketing strategy, make sure you thoroughly understand who or what makes an ideal client for your business.

- Always focus on the core way your business differentiates itself from every other business that does something similar.

- Strive to educate potential customers or clients, rather than simply "selling" to them. Show off your expertise and how your products or services can help your clients with challenges or problems they encounter.

- Incorporate your marketing strategy into your Web presence. Make sure your site is infused with education-based expertise that's easy to find when prospects search for products, services or solutions.

branding. Entrepreneurs, especially those in the start-up phase, might turn to any number of online sites to cheaply design their own logo and materials and order promotional products (T-shirts, pens, mugs, even Frisbees) at bulk rates with their company names splashed on them. Popular sites include www .logoyes. com (for do-it-yourself logos) and www.branders.com and www.cafepress.com (for promotional products).

Of course, marketing isn't just about a logo-emblazoned golf tee. Marketing is an ongoing process that's an essential part of creating your company's brand, growing its presence and winning customers. How you go about it is a true test of your own creativity and ingenuity. In this chapter, I'm including five strategies from entrepreneurs whose marketing approaches have struck me as particularly innovative or, in the case of Kate Spade, as counterintuitive. Their methods may not work for you or your company, but their smart strategies may inspire some brainstorming that can help you build your brand.

Strategy: Go Straight to the Customer
Richard Tait, cofounder, Cranium

Shortly after former Microsoft employee Richard Tait created the board game Cranium in 1998, he realized that his big marketing opportunity—the American International Toy Fair, an annual industry conference for manufacturers, distributors and sales agents where buying decisions are made—had come and gone. Disheartened, he and business partner Whit Alexander shuffled off to Starbucks to lament their lost opportunity. That's when they looked up and saw their potential customers— hip young adults—in line buying lattes. Inspiration struck: why not take their game to where their customers are, instead of the stores where games are normally sold? Cranium became the first game ever sold at Starbucks (Tait used his connections to persuade the coffee chain's CEO to stock it in stores). After that, the company inked more distribution deals, sold millions of games and ultimately was acquired by Hasbro in 2008 for $77.5 million.

The Cranium story illustrates a marketing basic: the importance of knowing your customers. It also demonstrates the true think-outside-the-box spirit that many successful entrepreneurs exhibit. For your industry, there may be a traditional marketing approach that every business owner takes to get products or services in front of customers. But is there potentially a better one? Or, if budget or other constraints prevent you from taking the usual approach, is there a new way you can reach your customers? When I interviewed Tait for a profile for SmartMoney.com, he described the Starbucks epiphany this way: "Often, a door that closes will result in some of your best creativity." The lesson: figure out who your customers are and how you can reach them, even if no one else has done that yet. And use your connections!

Strategy: Glorify the Weird

Paul Stremple, inventor, Banana Bunker

Necessity, of course, is the mother of invention, and when Paul Stremple's sister complained that her midday snack—a delicate banana—kept getting smushed in her briefcase, the trained architect put his design skills to use and came up with a solution. His invention, the Banana Bunker, is a transparent plastic container that mimics the shape of a banana and can be expanded or contracted to fit the fruit's size. With its suggestive shape (some might call it a fruit prophylactic) and functionality, the Banana Bunker pretty much sells itself, according to Stremple, in the Museum of Modern Art's gift store and others places around the world.

Stremple's story is one I can relate to as a journalist: highlight the unusual, bizarre or quirky and you'll win readers. While Stremple built his business around a rather unusual product, any company might play up a unique aspect to win customers. The trick is to do it without being too gimmicky. For instance, take the Hanger Bar & Boutique in New York, which would have been just like any other bar in the East Village except it also contained racks of vintage designer clothing for sale. Owners Natalka Burian and Betsy Nadel decided they needed a unique concept to stand out in a crowded market, and the designer duds won them press attention and positive reviews.

If you're worried your idea might be a little too oddball, conduct some informal market research. Throw a party and invite friends, family members or potential customers over to your house (or place of business) for a focus group on your concept. Supply food and beverages, and pay attention to what your critics say.

Strategy: Shoot for the Stars
Stacey Griffin, founder, Aqua2Go

When Stacy Griffin, a New Orleans mom, started a new business sell-ing eight-ounce boxes of purified water called Aqua2Go, she decided to seek some star power. Not only did she contact local media, but she sent samples of her products to about thirty television shows, such as Today, Live with Regis and Kelly *and* Oprah. *She got lucky: one sample went to comedian Ellen DeGeneres, who decided to feature the product on her daytime show.* Saturday Night Live *had just done a popular skit in which Justin Timberlake sang about a rather risqué gift in a box for his girlfriend. DeGeneres made up a similar jingle for Griffin's company, singing that customers need to "suck the straw in the box" of Aqua2Go. The response was immediate: Griffin got hun-dreds of messages from eager customers, plus interest from large gro-cery chains. Her product is now sold in Whole Foods, Wal-Mart and other stores.*

Griffin's story illustrates that a few moments in the lime-light can go a long way. A business owner who manages to get his or her products mentioned on a TV show or used by a celeb-rity can see a sudden, measurable jump in demand. While it's a bit like winning the lottery, hooking a celeb fan isn't impossi-ble. If landing a TV show is what you seek, try contacting show producers to see if you can send them your product. You can also use the services of a product placement firm to get your hand-crafted earrings or bottle of organic lotion into goodie bags at a celebrity event. (Check the firm's credentials, though, as not all are reputable.)

An easier, more realistic way to generate buzz is simply to try to win publicity from your local news outlet, or perhaps a national publication. Some businesses hire publicists; others do it themselves by writing press releases and distributing them, for a fee, via press release distributions services such as PRWeb.com and MyPRGenie.com.

Strategy: Rule the Internet
Gary Vaynerchuk, owner, Wine Library

Gary Vaynerchuk turned his family business, a small liquor store in Springfield, New Jersey, into one of the highest-grossing independently owned retailers in the country thanks to a number of splashy endeavors on the Web. In 2006, Vaynerchuk began hosting daily video tastings on the store's website, swirling wine around in a glass and shouting colorful descriptions, such as "I get gorgeous bacon fat ripping through my nose right off the bat!" while sniffing a French Burgundy. He also hosts an online forum, invites viewers to send him questions via Facebook, and utilizes platforms such as Digg, Delicious and Twitter so that fans can share or vote on content. Vaynerchuk, who refers to himself as a "social media sommelier," attributes the company's success (sales have shot to about $50 million a year, from $4 million) to his Web 2.0 brand building.

While some business owners may be slow to embrace the Internet, Vaynerchuk has given it a bear hug. And while much of his ability to connect to customers has a lot to do with his colorful—some might say over-the-top—personality, his decision to attack and conquer multiple Internet platforms has put him in a sweet spot revenuewise.

More consumers are logging on to shop and to surf for reviews that influence their buying decisions, so it's smart for entrepreneurs in a variety of industries to grab customers through online marketing. Business owner E. B. Moss, who runs a marketing agency in New York, confessed to me that joining online sites such as Facebook seemed foreign (at least at first) because, as a person in her forties, she could still remember the smell of ink from mimeograph machines. But she's not one to turn down a challenge, and she's not only created a Facebook profile (on which she routinely posts news stories, videos and updates about her business) but also has started a blog and sends out an e-mail newsletter to clients. While the results aren't as dramatic as Vaynerchuk's, she's found it an effective way to communicate with clients and win new business.

Strategy: Ignore Copycats
Kate Spade, designer

Handbag maker Kate Spade has parlayed good taste and a penchant for simple, boxy bags into a multimillion-dollar fashion powerhouse. When she and husband Andy were just starting out, they joked about places like New York's Canal Street, where knockoff designer bags are sold on the cheap, and how funny it would be if her bags became popular enough to rip off. A few years later, it was no laughing matter. Not only were Kate Spade knockoffs being sold on the street for a fraction of the price, but the designs were nothing like her true style. While Spade worked with authorities to try to curb the abuse, she says the best thing she did was to ignore the knockoffs. Instead, she focused on what she could control: making products her loyal customers would love. In 1999, Neiman Marcus paid $33.6 million for a majority interest in her company, ultimately selling it to Liz Claiborne in 2006 for $120 million.

What I like about Spade's story is its surprisingly simple message: don't waste time worrying about the competition when you should be focused instead on managing your brand. Particularly if you're in an industry such as fashion, copycats can actually help spread your ideas as a trend—making your brand even more valuable to brand-conscious consumers. Clearly, it's wise to protect your idea with patents, copyrights or trademarks (for more on that, see the box on page 140). But a mistake too many entrepreneurs make—especially those who develop unique products or services—is to spend too much time and energy protecting the idea, while dropping the ball on marketing.

That's what happened to Curt Todd, who admits to worrying too much about imitators when he and his wife, Sue, developed MailWraps, which are decorative mailbox covers. The

HOW TO PROTECT YOUR BRILLIANT IDEA

You want to spread the word about your business. But you also want to keep your innovative product or clever brand name safe from rivals, counterfeiters or rip-off artists.

What to do? Safeguarding your company's intellectual property through patents, trademarks or copyrights will allow you to seek damages, a big deterrent to imitators. Here's a brief overview of all three types of protection:

Patents. Issued by the U.S. Patent and Trademark Office (USPTO), a patent is easily the most expensive—and most valuable—protection for an entrepreneur with a innovative product or business method. A patent essentially gives you a mini-monopoly for twenty years. The application process can be a bit complicated, so it's wise to use the services of a patent attorney. Costs generally range from $2,000 to $10,000, depending on complexity.

Trademarks. A word, symbol, logo or image that identifies a product or service can be trademarked, as can a scent, sound or color (such as Tiffany Blue). There are more than forty classes of goods and services, and you can register a trademark (for a fee) in more than one category. A pastry shop ower, for instance, could register a trademark in both the food class (in the goods category) and the restaurant class (in the services category). You can conduct a free search to see if a mark is already registered on the USPTO's Web site using the Trademark Electronic Search System. The filing fee is $375 if done by paper and $275 to $325 if done electronically.

Copyright. A copyright protects original works, such as poetry, novels, movies, songs, computer software and architectural designs. A business, for instance, might want a copyright to protect its training manual. Original works on a website (such as writings, artwork or photos) may be copyrighted. Copyright law does not protect domain names; instead, the nonprofit Internet Corporation for Assigned Names and Numbers handles domain name system management. The fee for a basic copyright registration is $45 when you submit a paper application, or you can lower that fee by filing through the U.S. Copyright Office's online system for $35.

Keep in mind that if you plan on selling or distributing your products abroad, you should consider filing with those countries' intellectual property protection authorities in addition to those in the United States.

couple says they spent way too much money developing expensive packaging (to distinguish their quirky new product from any possible knockoffs) and not enough time simply talking to customers about the purpose of MailWraps. When they shifted the focus, they won customers—and lots of them. The former home-based business posted $5 million in sales in 2006 and has since moved into a 51,000-square-foot building.

ALWAYS BE NETWORKING

In business, as they say, it's not what you know but whom you know.

Networking is one of the most valuable (and inexpensive) forms of marketing. Many successful business owners are master networkers who can walk into a room full of strangers, make a connection and handily attract a new client, partner or investor.

While it helps to be naturally outgoing, networking is a skill that can be learned. First, it's necessary to get yourself in the right spot—and that means interacting with people who can potentially help your business. Attend a conference, trade show or social event where you can meet people who either need your product or service or know someone who might. Consider throwing the party yourself at your home, your place of business or a local bar or restaurant.

WOMEN AND MINORITY ENTREPRENEURS

A unique marketing tool for women and minority entrepreneurs is something called certification. Here's the gist: a growing number of companies (typically, big corporations such as Procter and Gamble, PepsiCo, Wal-Mart, IBM, Marriott and others) want to better connect with customers who are women or minorities. These companies have decided, as a strategy, to set aside millions of dollars in vendor and procurement contracts for small businesses that have been certified as minority- or woman-owned. This is often referred to as "supplier diversity." Some corporations also specifically want to work with entrepreneurs who are veterans, disabled, or lesbian or gay.

The logic is that by supporting diverse small businesses, these big companies can make inroads into untapped markets or improve their reputations in certain communities. For the right certified business, that can mean access to a lucrative contract. Certification certainly doesn't guarantee a contract, but it can boost your company's visibility among decision makers in big corporations' supply chains.

To become certified, an entrepreneur must submit financial records such as tax returns, bank documents and a profit-and-loss statement, and provide proof of majority ownership by a minority or woman. Eligibility is usually determined after interviews and site visits. The two biggest certifying bodies—the National Minority Supplier Development Council and the Women's Business Enterprise National Council—each provide certification (usually for a fee of $200 to $500, depending on the small business's size and location). Both agencies provide information on certified businesses to purchasing managers through online databases.

The SBA and some state and local government agencies also certify woman- and minority-owned enterprises, often through programs for what they call "economically or socially disadvantaged" businesses.

For more information, visit these websites:

National Minority Supplier Development Council
www.nmsdcus.org
The NMSDC certifies and matches more than 15,000 minority-owned businesses (Asian, black, Hispanic and Native American) with 3,500 corporations, universities and hospitals that want to purchase goods and services. To qualify, the business must be at least 51 percent minority-owned, -operated and

-controlled. The NMSDC has a national office in New York and thirty-nine affiliates across the country.

Women's Business Enterprise National Council
www.wbenc.com
WBENC certifies 8,000 woman-owned businesses with more than 1,000 major corporations across the country and also a number of federal and government agencies. To qualify, the business must be 51 percent owned and controlled by a woman or women, and provide proof of effective management of the company. WBENC has fourteen partner organizations across the country that handle WBENC certification in all fifty states.

National Gay and Lesbian Chamber of Commerce
www.nglcc.org
The NGLCC's Supplier Diversity Initiative certifies lesbian-, gay-, bisexual- and/or transgender-owned business enterprises (LGBTBEs) and works to provide opportunities for LGBTBEs to gain exposure within the corporate procurement process.

SBA's 8(a) and SDB Business Development
www.sba.gov/aboutsba/sbaprograms/8abd/index.html
As discussed in Chapter 7, the SBA administers two programs for what it terms "socially and economically disadvantaged" businesses. Members of certain minority groups automatically qualify; business owners who are socially disadvantaged because of ethnicity, gender, physical handicap or location may also qualify. To be considered economically disadvantaged, individuals must have a net worth of less than $250,000, excluding the value of the business and personal residence. Certification may improve a business's ability to compete for government contracts.

U.S. Department of Veteran Affairs Center for Veterans Enterprise
http://www.vetbiz.gov
The center can register a business as veteran owned for free as long it is 51 percent owned by one or more veterans or service-disabled veterans. That can help a business win government contracts that may be set aside for veteran-owned businesses.

How to get the conversation flowing without sounding overly aggressive? Here are some tips.

Forget the artificial sales pitch.

Keep the conversation natural. Share information about you and your company, but not in a way that's canned. Asking other people questions about themselves, too, creates opportunities to share what you're doing without the conversation seeming like it's all about me-me-me.

Communicate your passion.

Not only can you win people over with your enthusiasm for your product or service, but an upbeat manner is often contagious. Getting other people to share their passion, too, helps create a memorable two-way conversation.

Don't commandeer the conversation.

The most successful networkers are charismatic people who make the person they're speaking to feel special. Look other people in the eye, really listen to what they have to say and guide them to topics they want to talk about.

Keep in touch.

You'll likely end up exchanging business cards—but that's where this new relationship starts, not ends. Make sure to call or send follow-up e-mails or notes with a reminder about what you can do for them.

CHAPTER 14

HIRING EMPLOYEES

W hen you can't run your business by yourself, it's time to hire your first employees.

Becoming a boss—not just of yourself but of others—requires leadership skills, fiscal responsibility and a certain finesse when it comes to dealing with people. Take a management course, chat with a mentor or consult with other business owners to get a better idea of what works and what doesn't. Entrepreneurs often credit their company's success to their hardworking employees; it's human nature that people will perform best for a boss who can communicate his or her vision, motivate with incentives and treat workers with respect, so it's important that you develop the skills to be an effective boss.

Once you're prepared to take on the responsibility of being a boss, there are a few basics to consider before you begin hiring staff.

Make sure, first and foremost, that you can afford to pay employees' salaries on a regular and ongoing basis. Making payroll is one of the biggest worries—and sources of stress—for business owners. To make sure you don't come up short, you must be confident in and have a good knowledge of your company's cash flow, which we covered in Chapter 9.

Setting salaries itself is a delicate task. You don't want to pay someone too little, as you may not attract or retain the best talent. On the other hand, paying too much for your employees can strain your bottom line. To come up with the best figure, it's a good idea to define exactly what work the person will be performing for you and whether you need that person to work part-time or full-time. Then do some research. Check with your trade association about competitive salaries for that line of work. Ask business owners in similar industries what they pay employees (if you don't feel comfortable asking a competitor for this information, check employment listings in the local paper or online to see what they're offering job candidates). Sites such as Salary.com and GlassDoor.com also provide information on salaries in various industries. You'll want to know whether competitors provide health insurance, retirement plans, bonuses or other benefits. Your accountant may have an idea of typical pay in your industry or area and can help you determine how much of your budget should be dedicated to payroll. You may wish to come up with a minimum/maximum salary that you afford to pay, so you can adjust your offer based on the candidate's skills and experience.

As an alternative to hiring employees, you might consider retaining independent contractors, who work as needed. Sites such as eLance.com and Guru.com can help you find freelance Web designers, programmers and other professionals. A growing number of business owners are also turning to virtual assistants for extra help, which might be all you need, especially if you're looking for someone to handle administrative tasks. You can search for one through the International Virtual Assistants Association, at www.ivaa.org.

Last, review all the pertinent legal and financial information regarding employees. I recommend consulting with an attorney or accountant about withholding taxes, paying overtime and providing meal breaks. And if you're a home-based business, familiarize yourself with local zoning laws, to make sure you're not running afoul of regulation by having a non-family-member employee working out of your home.

HIRING THE BEST

As you begin recruiting and interviewing employees, you'll obviously be drawn to certain candidates because of their experience, educational background and personality. While it's easy to make a decision based on what you see in front of you, it's wise to consider what may be hidden from view, too.

Small businesses, unfortunately, are particularly vulnerable to embezzlement and other kinds of employee theft because they lack the checks and balances of big corporations. One report by the Association of Certified Fraud Examiners found that the median loss for small firms with fewer than one hundred employees was $190,000. The most common schemes? Employees fraudulently writing company checks, skimming revenues and processing phony invoices.

You can increase your chances of avoiding problems—and spotting dishonesty—by beefing up your hiring practices. Here's how to do it.

- **Use a formal job application.** Take a page from corporate America's book and supply job candidates with an application that requests full name, address, education, employment record (with years) and references. An application that includes all of this information can give you a clearer picture of someone's background than, say, a resume that he or she provides. Also, it's wise to state on the application that supplying false information can lead to dismissal. (Documentation can help protect you in the event of an employee lawsuit; for more on that, see the section on page 150, "Avoiding Employee Lawsuits.")

- **Ask tough questions.** Carefully review the application, and during the in-person interview, ask probing questions, especially about gaps in employment. A candidate may certainly have any number of innocent explanations (such as attending school, reevaluating his or her career or caring for a child or other family member), but gaps between jobs can indicate an inability to hold down a position, a sudden dismissal or, at worst, a prison stay. Arrange for others at your company (or a trusted advisor, if you're a solo entrepreneur) to meet the person as well; getting a second or third opinion to confirm your impressions will help you make more solid hiring decisions.

- **Call former employers and check references.** Often, former bosses don't want to provide too much negative information, for fear that they could be sued for defamation. At the least, you should be able to verify the person's employment history and salary history. The best question to ask a former employer is simply, "Is this person eligible for rehire?" If the answer is no, that's a definite red flag.

- **Perform a background check.** Preemployment checks can screen out applicants who may be unfit (or dangerous) for your workplace because of a criminal record. Some states may require that employers in certain industries—say, child care or health care—conduct background checks. A background check also can confirm the accuracy of information that the candidate provided on the application. While a background check isn't necessary for all employees, it's smart to conduct one on a job candidate who will have access to sensitive data or your company's finances. The Fair Credit Reporting Act, which sets standards for employment screening, requires that you get consent from a potential employee before conducting a background check. Check the FTC's website to make sure you are in compliance (www.ftc.gov/os/statutes/fcrajump.shtm). Also, you don't want to run afoul of state or federal laws concerning the kinds of information an employer uses to make employment decisions. If you do perform a background check, ask a business owner or your attorney for a referral to a reputable firm.

- **Invite a potential hire for a paid tryout.** You can learn a lot about potential employees, including how well they fit into your small business environment, by inviting them to work on a test project or spending a trial run in your office. A tryout may be a particularly good way to test an applicant's technical skills—say, a proficiency with a type of software—and may reveal far more than a reference or background check.

MAKING THE OFFER

Once you've found your perfect candidate, you'll want to make an offer he or she can't refuse. Unfortunately, small businesses typically can't offer the generous packages of benefits and stock options that large corporations can (for more on that, see Chapter 15). But as a small business, you'll likely have a powerful weapon when it comes to recruiting or retaining employees: flexibility.

Unlike large corporations, which are still struggling to figure out the best ways to offer flexible scheduling, small businesses are doing it with relative ease. That's often because the business owner is a former corporate employee who disliked the rigid policies of his or her former employer and wants to rewrite the rules.

Research from the Families and Work Institute, a New York group that studies workplace issues, has found that small businesses with fifty to ninety-nine employees are significantly more likely than large companies with a thousand or more workers to allow employees to change start and stop hours on a daily basis (17 percent versus 4 percent), return to work gradually after childbirth or adoption (66 percent versus 49 percent) and gradually phase into retirement (25 percent versus 14 percent).

Additionally, a growing number of small businesses are allowing employees to adjust their work hours, work from home or even share jobs with coworkers. In surveys, flexible scheduling invariably ranks right near the top (after higher salaries) as one of the most sought-after workplace changes, particularly for employees caring for a young child, a special-needs child or an aging relative. In addition, younger people who are part of the "millennial" generation born between 1980 and 1995, who have grown up with the Internet and the ability to work anywhere (and anytime), are more eager to work for companies that can promise flexibility.

Consider David A. Fields of Ridgefield, Connecticut, who wanted to start a management consulting firm. Fields knew his staff would have to be highly trained, well educated and accustomed to working with big-name clients. The problem: he couldn't offer pricey health insurance, plush office space (his company is home based) or any other type of fancy corporate benefits that such seasoned professionals might expect. The solution? Offer prospective employees the ability to work remotely.

The result has been a "fabulous" staff of six independent contractors—all of whom are raising kids or caring for elderly parents—who work out of their homes and stay connected to Fields's company, Ascendant Consulting, through Web applications such as an online meeting service and an Internet phone system.

There are, of course, a few drawbacks. Every so often, it seems like more could be accomplished if they were all sitting in the same room together. "I can't walk down the hall and kick someone in the shins or give them a big hug," Fields says with a laugh. But the ability to attract key talent who want to telecommute from any part of the country, all while devoting time to family, is worth any inconvenience. "I try to find the very best people in the country at what they do, and make them part of my team," says Fields. "You can't do that with a traditional business."

AVOIDING EMPLOYEE LAWSUITS

Small business owners might be surprised to learn they they are vulnerable to the same worker complaints that plague

SMALL COMPANIES HELP
EMPLOYEES STRIKE A BALANCE

In addition to increased flexibility, small companies also find it easier to offer inexpensive work-life programs. The Alfred P. Sloan Awards, which honor companies with innovative work environments, has highlighted these companies for the following efforts:

- Worktank, a Seattle advertising agency with seventy-five employees, for providing ways for staff to manage stress. The company has a lounge equipped with Nintendo Wii gaming consoles, where workers can blow off some steam, and hosts "Social Friday" office gatherings, where workers can kick back with food and beverages. As an added plus, Worktank also allows pet owners to bring their dogs into work, as long as they're well behaved and on a leash.

- Cachet Homes, a Scottsdale, Arizona, home builder with fifty employees, for allowing staff a nice perk: early dismissals on Fridays. The company has reconfigured its normal 8 a.m.–5 p.m. hours during the summers so that staff work from 7:45 a.m. to 5:15 p.m. Mondays thru Thursday and leave at 1:00 p.m. on Friday. The program has been so popular that the company does a holiday version, allowing staff to leave at 3:00 p.m. on Fridays in December.

- Cooper Roberts Simonsen, an architectural firm with sixty-eight employees in Salt Lake City, for paying for tuition, education or skill development. The company picks up the tab (up to $2,000 per semester) for graduate- or undergraduate-level classes, and also awards annual travel scholarships to employees who wish to study architecture in various spots in the world. Employees must apply for the scholarships and be chosen by a committee; scholarships cover up to $2,000 in expenses, plus time off. So far, recipients have studied intergenerational housing in Germany; art and architecture in Cambridge, England; and indigenous designs in Hawaii.

Companies that win Alfred P. Sloan Awards must show that their unconventional benefits have enhanced their workplaces and helped them retain quality staff.

corporate America. In particular, more employees are suing companies for violating wage-and-hour rules, typically claiming they weren't paid overtime. A small business that lacks in-house counsel or a human resources department can unwittingly violate federal or state laws covering workplaces. And many business owners, eager to create informal workplaces, simply neglect to educate staff on harassment or discrimination policies. The following steps will help you avoid a potentially devastating employee lawsuit:

Classify employees properly.
Workers are either "exempt" or "nonexempt" from wage-and-hour laws based on duties and salaries. Historically, employees who can practice independent judgment, such as those in executive, professional or administrative positions, are exempt. Employees who are paid an hourly wage, generally, are considered nonexempt and must receive at least the minimum wage and overtime pay. Check the Department of Labor's online Wage and Hour Division for more information.

Maintain an antidiscrimination and harassment policy.
Make it clear via a written policy given to employees at their time of hire that certain behavior is unacceptable, namely, unlawful harassment or discrimination based on age, gender, race, religion and other factors not related to the quality of a person's work. Consult an attorney about what your state requires. Include those polices in your employee handbook (see the box "Developing a Formal Employee Handbook" on page 153 for how to do that).

Document, document, document.
Conduct performance reviews, and don't sugarcoat bad performance. Keep a written record of any unacceptable workplace behavior, such as distasteful conduct, extended absences or insufficient work. Put employees on notice, and give them

DEVELOPING A FORMAL EMPLOYEE HANDBOOK

A useful tool for any growing company is the employee handbook, which outlines your policies on harassment, discrimination and discipline, and can serve as a shield in the event an employment claim is brought against your business. A handbook can also communicate your vision of the company to employees, and provide exact details on how you expect them to perform their jobs, treat customers and carry out the company's goals.

Most companies develop an employee handbook in the growth phase, when they have hired ten or more employees. To learn how to develop one, search for "employee handbook" on www.sba.gov, or check sites such as SCORE or CCH's Business Owner's Toolkit. A free template is available on Business.gov, the government's site that helps small businesses understand legal requirements, at www.business.gov/business-law/employment/hiring/employee-handbook.html.

After you draft a handbook, make sure you have it reviewed by an attorney familiar with employment law. Your handbook should contain a disclaimer clearly stating that it's not a legal contract (that way you're free to end someone's employment at will). While I recommend developing an employee handbook, at the least you should have a short written document that outlines your general work policies (such as your antidiscrimination and harassment policy), and be sure to have employees read (and sign) that document when they are hired.

Most handbooks contain this information:

- A basic overview of the company, including its mission statement

- A list of products and services offered

- An organizational chart

- Standard policies on hours of work, paid holidays, vacation, conduct, dress code, promotions and overtime

- A section on harassment and discrimination, drug and alcohol use, employee safety and use of company property

- A section on retirement plans and health care benefits, if applicable

an opportunity to improve. Legal experts say workers who are surprised by termination are more likely to sue.

WHEN IT'S NOT WORKING OUT

At one time or another, as a business owner you'll probably have to deal with a problem employee who underperforms or violates one of the rules you've outlined in your employee handbook. Your first course of action, as outlined in Chapter 10, is to talk privately with the employee, adjust the job as need be, and give him or her time to improve performance. As discussed, make sure to document unacceptable behavior. If your employee fails to improve after repeated warnings (as a general rule of thumb, allow for three), then it's time to let that person go.

Provided there is no contract or collective bargaining agreement, most hiring is presumed to be "at will"—meaning you're free to discharge the employee for any reason (and he or she is equally free to quit). Still, check with your attorney or state Department of Labor to make sure you're not violating any employment laws. You may wish to draw up a severance agreement, which outlines any compensation or continued benefits the person may receive after termination, and have that ready for your final meeting.

Once you've made the decision to fire, arrange to meet with the employee in person, in either a conference room or another private setting. Explain briefly why you're unsatisfied with his or her performance, and refer to the documented unacceptable behavior. Allow the person to respond, but be clear: the decision has been made, and it's final. Avoid attempts to engage in discussion or reconsideration. Tell the person to gather his or her personal belongings, return any company property (such as keys, security ID, credit card or electronic devices) and leave the premises.

CHAPTER 15

Benefits: Health Care and Retirement

If you've ever worked for a large employer, chances are your initial days on the job included a brief seminar by the human resources department on the health and retirements benefits now available to you.

It goes without saying that starting a business is a much different story. Unfortunately, nothing dampens entrepreneurial spirit more than the thought of paying for benefits—for yourself and your staff—and dealing with all the paperwork involved in setting up and managing such programs. The good news is that more resources than ever are now available to business owners, which we'll go over in this chapter, starting with health care.

HEALTH CARE

There's no getting around it: health care is expensive. In fact, in good economic times and in bad, the cost and availability of health insurance consistently ranks as the number one concern for small business owners.

Entrepreneurs looking to curb costs have limited options. Some are fortunate enough to be able to latch on to a spouse's employer-sponsored insurance (I've even heard of self-employed individuals getting or staying married for this dubious reason, which I don't recommend). Many opt for catastrophic insurance, paying a low premium but a high deductible for coverage of major hospital and medical expenses. And then others— especially those who are young and healthy—simply go without health insurance, a risky strategy that can backfire easily if they become sick or injured.

Organizations such as the National Federation of Independent Business and the National Small Business Administration consistently lobby on Capitol Hill for better access to health care for small businesses. There have been some developments in recent years, thanks to greater awareness of the challenges that business owners face in obtaining coverage for themselves, their families and their employees. One of the most notable is the federal government's creation in 2003 of health savings accounts or HSAs, which provide a tax-advantaged way for business owners and employees to accumulate savings for medical expenses.

In this section, we'll take a look at health care choices for business owners, whether you're a sole proprietor who only wants health coverage for yourself or an owner of a small but growing business who wants to offer health benefits as a way to recruit or retain talented employees.

For the Solo Entrepreneur

Getting health care on your own is a bit daunting, and the options vary depending on the state in which you live. (For more state-specific information, check with your state's insurance office.) If you're used to an employer picking up the majority of the cost, get ready for some sticker shock. Here's a rundown of your basic options:

COBRA

Have you recently left an employer who's provided you with health insurance, or are you considering it? It may make sense to extend your coverage through the federal Consolidated Omnibus Budget Reconciliation Act, or COBRA.

To be eligible for COBRA coverage, you must have been enrolled in your former employer's health plan when you worked there, and the health plan must continue to be in effect for active employees, according to the Department of Labor, which provides information about COBRA on its website at www.dol.gov/dol/topic/health-plans/cobra.htm. You can generally extend coverage at group rates for up to eighteen months after leaving a job, although be warned: it isn't cheap. The monthly tab is equal to the full cost of your group health coverage, plus a 2 percent administrative fee, which typically comes out to about $400 for individuals and $1,000 for families. If you have a preexisting medical condition (such as cancer, diabetes or other chronic illnesses), COBRA can be a particularly attractive option, as it allows you to stay continuously covered by health insurance while searching for a new insurance plan. That ensures there isn't a gap in coverage; the Health Insurance Portability and Accountability Act, or HIPAA, requires insurers to provide coverage regardless of a person's health status so long as there isn't a gap of more than sixty-three days between your insurance plans.

Group plans

It's not impossible to qualify for a group health insurance plan, even if you work by yourself. The benefit of joining a group plan is that you'll generally have access to better coverage than an individual policy, at a lower premium. In some states, a self-employed person can buy health insurance at a group rate under what's known as a group-of-one plan. Check with your state insurance office for eligibility criteria and participation rules.

You should also check with industry groups, professional associations, and local chambers of commerce as an alternative route to accessing group coverage. For instance, the New York–based Freelancers Union, which represents freelancers, consultants, contractors and other independent workers, offers its members access to discounted health insurance through its group plan. In 2009, for example, a member in New York City could choose from a variety of preferred provider organization (PPO) plans at a monthly cost ranging from $257 to $455 for individuals and $753 to $1,323 for families. The same group also offers high-deductible plans, including one with a $10,000 annual deductible that is priced at $141 a month for individuals and $466 for families.

IF YOU'RE DENIED COVERAGE

People seeking health insurance on the private market are also more likely to be denied coverage due to their health status. If you are turned down for private insurance because of a preexisting condition, you may be able to join your state's high-risk health insurance pool, which provides coverage to individuals with serious conditions. Premiums vary, and waiting periods may apply. Check with your state's insurance office, or the National Association of State Comprehensive Health Insurance Plans at www.naschip.org.

Individual health insurance

If you can't join a group plan, or if you want the freedom to customize policies to your own personal health situation, you might elect individual coverage via the private market. Rates will vary based on your age, your health, the region of the country you live in and whether you're electing individual or family coverage. If you're in relatively good health, you can minimize the cost by reducing the level of coverage—for instance, you can cut out coverage for office visits or prescription drugs—and you can lower premiums by raising the deductible. A 2004 study by the Kaiser Family Foundation, based on data provided by online vendor eHealthInsurance, found that individual monthly premiums were generally lower than those of group plans, but the benefits were much more modest. To compare policies, check out sites such as www.eHealth Insurance.com, or search for a local agent in your area at the National Association of Health Underwriters site at www .nahu.org.

Health savings accounts

An HSA is an alternative to traditional health insurance, and essentially has two parts: a high-deductible insurance policy and a portable savings account into which you contribute pre-tax dollars to pay for medical expenses not covered by the high-deductible plan, such as medications and routine office visits. HSAs "roll over" from year to year, so you can potentially accumulate savings that can be used, tax-free, to pay for medical costs in retirement. One drawback: HSAs may not be appropriate if you're older or chronically ill, as frequent doctor visits and health care expenses can easily eat up the money in the account. The minimum deductible amount to be eligible for an HSA in 2009 is $1,150 for individuals and $2,300 for families, with a maximum contribution amount of $3,000 for individuals and $5,950 for families. If you're fifty-five or older, a catch-up provision allows you to add an extra $1,000 to your account. For more details, check out www.HSAfinder .com, a good online source for independent HSA information. To shop or compare plans, check www.hsainsider.com.

Health Care for Employees

As your business starts to grow and you hire employees, you'll gain a competitive edge in attracting a more qualified staff if you offer health benefits. Unfortunately, many small companies are unable to provide coverage under traditional group plans—such as an HMO (health maintenance organization), PPO (preferred provider organization), or POS (point of service) health plan—because of the steep cost.

For traditional health insurance coverage at smaller firms with fewer than two hundred employees, the average annual premium is $4,553 for singles (that's $379 a month) and $11,835 for families ($986 a month), according to a 2007 survey on employer benefits by the Kaiser Family Foundation and Health Research and Educational Trust. The employer portion at small firms, on average, amounts to $3,992 ($333 a month) and $7,599 ($633 a month) respectively. While nearly all large businesses with at least two hundred workers offer health benefits to their workers, fewer than half of the smallest firms with three to nine workers do so, the Kaiser/HRET survey found.

If you're considering starting a health insurance plan for your employees, research what your competition is doing to set some benchmarks for yourself. If you want to offer a traditional plan, you might keep costs lower by asking employees to share a larger portion of the premium burden. Some small companies provide a minimum amount of coverage and allow employees to pay more for richer plans.

For a growing number of companies, trying HSAs makes financial sense; it effectively puts more of the onus on the employee to pay for medical expenses. In a 2008 survey of six thousand small business owners by Information Strategies, a firm that tracks HSAs, one-third said they now provide HSAs—and half said the plans were easier to administer than their old plans.

In figuring out which approach best suits the needs of your company, your employees *and* your

---

AN ALTERNATIVE TO THE GROUP PLAN

Tim Lesko, president of Greenco Environmental, an organic recycling company in Barnesville, Georgia, shopped around for a group health plan for his five employees but decided it would be cheaper for the start-up company to partially reimburse staff members' individual policies, which they set up on their own. Now the company picks up 75 percent of the cost of an employee's health care premium (up to $200 a month), while the employee pays the remaining 25 percent plus all copays and deductibles. "In difficult economic times, my small business providing [any] health care for its employees is seen as a benefit," Lesko says, "and people feel more appreciated for it being provided."

ARE HEALTH CARE COSTS DEDUCTIBLE?

Yes, the cost of health care coverage for yourself and your employees is a deductible business expense.

However, a self-employed individual must calculate his or her own self-employment tax before taking that deduction. Remember, a self-employed person pays two different forms of taxes—regular income tax plus the self-employment tax (or the full amount of Social Security and Medicare taxes that normally are split between an employer and an employee). This applies to sole proprietors, partners in partnerships, LLC owners and S corporation owners.

Organizations such as the National Federation of Independence Business and the National Association for the Self-Employed support a change in the tax code that would allow entrepreneurs to first deduct the cost of health insurance before calculating their self-employment taxes.

budget, you may want to tap the services of a benefits consultant or an insurance broker, who can help you sort through the choices. That's how Nancy Mobley, founder of the human resources firm Insight Performance in Dedham, Massachusetts, chose a health plan for her twenty-five employees. After working with a broker, she settled on an HMO plan with a monthly premium of $475 for individuals and $950 for family coverage. Her company picks up 75 percent of the cost for individuals and 50 percent for families. "We believe that the outlay is necessary to remain competitive, although we are just a small company," she says. You can search for a broker through the National Association of Health Underwriters or ask other business owners for a referral. You can also compare small business group plans on eHealthInsurance's site, at www.ehealthinsurance.com/ehi/small-business-group-health-insurance.ds.

RETIREMENT

When you become your own boss, you have an array of tax-advantaged retirement plans to choose from that are relatively simple and cheap to set up. Most plans allow you to build a nest egg while saving on business and personal incomes taxes, too.

What's right for you depends on how much you can contribute. If you're not yet at the point where you can sock away sizable chunks, then consider basic options designed for individuals, such as the Roth or traditional IRA.

Roth IRA

With a Roth IRA, annual contributions are made with after-tax dollars, up to $5,000 per person ($6,000 if you are age fifty or older). Beginning in 2010, the contribution limit will adjust annually for inflation in $500 increments. While you don't get the immediate tax deduction with a Roth IRA, you do get flexibility: after five years, contributions can be withdrawn before age fifty-nine and a half with no penalty. If you're a business owner with inconsistent income, that means you can simultaneously save for retirement without losing the ability to access the cash—tax-free and penalty-free—if the need arises. Contributions to Roth IRAs are limited based on income, however. If you're a single filer, the amount you can contribute begins to phase out once your income exceeds $105,000 and ends completely at $120,000; for married filers, the phase-out range is $166,000 to $176,000.

Traditional IRA

Another basic popular option is the traditional IRA, which has the same annual contribution limits as the Roth IRA, with the added bonus that contributions are normally tax deductible in the tax year made. Generally, if you do not participate in an employer-sponsored retirement plan, then your contributions are fully deductible, regardless of your adjusted gross income. Your deduction can be limited if you're married and your spouse participates in an employer-sponsored retirement plan; in that case, your deduction is based on your adjusted gross income level. The traditional IRA doesn't have the same flexibility as the Roth. If you withdraw money early, you generally have to pay income taxes and a 10 percent penalty, except for special circumstances, such as the purchase of a first home. For more details, see *SmartMoney*'s online IRA primer at www.smartmoney.com/personal-finance/retirement/an-ira-primer-7957.

BEYOND BASICS

Once you're past the start-up years and drawing a comfortable salary, it's time to look at options beyond IRAs, designed specifically for business owners. Keep in mind that once your business has employees, these plans generally mandate that you cover them if you have a plan for yourself. That's a great tool for recruiting and retaining employees, but you'll need to consider how much room you have in the budget for contributions. If you have employees, you should consult a small business financial advisor or benefits consultant before selecting a retirement plan. Some good places to start shopping for information:

Charles Schwab Small Business Retirement Plans
www.schwab.com/public/schwab/home/account_types/small
_business_retirement

Fidelity Small Business Retirement Plans
http://personal.fidelity.com/products/retirement/getstart/
newacc/smallbizintro.shtml.cvsr

Vanguard Small Business Investments and Retirement Plans
https://personal.vanguard.com/us/accounttypes/smallbusiness

T. Rowe Price Small Business Retirement Plans
http://individual.troweprice.com/public/Retail/Retirement/
Small-Business-Retirement-Plans

Principal Financial Group For Businesses
www.principal.com/biz.htm

Here's a rundown of some of the best options, based on 2009 rules:

SIMPLE IRA

The SIMPLE (Savings Incentive Match Plan for Employees) IRA is a low-cost plan that's designed for businesses with one hundred or fewer employees. It's easy to set up, and there's no IRS filing. With the SIMPLE IRA, the maximum annual contribution is $11,500, which grows tax deferred. The plan allows employees to fund their own accounts, and as the employer you're required to match their contributions, up to 3 percent of employee compensation.

SEP IRA

If you want to make more sizable contributions for yourself and your employees, a SEP (Simplified Employee Pension) might be more appropriate. The SEP allows for contributions of up to 20 percent of self-employment income (25 percent if you're an employee of your own corporation), up to as much as $49,000 for the plan year. The SEP also requires no IRS filing and is simple to establish. The percentage that you contribute into your account can vary from year to year, but keep in mind that you must contribute the same percentage into your eligible employees' accounts, based on their compensation. Employees aren't allowed to make their own contributions.

401(k)

The 401(k) isn't just for corporate America. If you're a solo entrepreneur, you can set up your own plan—referred to as a solo, individual or self-employed 401(k)—and contribute up to $16,500 of your compensation annually, or $22,000 if you are fifty or older. An extra bonus: your business can make an additional tax-deductible contribution of up to 25 percent of your compensation (slightly less if you are a sole proprietor or unincorporated). The maximum total contribution is $49,000 per year, or $54,500 if you are fifty or older. And your contribution amount is flexible, so you can make higher contributions when business is good.

If you've got staff, you can set up a business 401(k) plan relatively cheaply, although you'll have to pay administrative fees. You can generally customize a plan to suit your business. A traditional plan might allow employees to make pretax contributions (again, at the maximum level of $16,500 per year) through payroll deductions, while you as the employer can decide at your own discretion whether to provide a match. For instance, you might match 50 percent of employees' contributions, up to 6 percent of their salaries.

Defined benefit plan

A defined benefit plan is essentially your own pension plan. If you're an older business owner—say, in your fifties or so—and you haven't stashed away a lot in retirement savings, a DB plan allows you to catch up quickly. Your contributions are based on how much is needed to give you a specific payout in retirement; that payout can be as high as $195,000 a year. You'll need the services of an actuary to calculate your contributions, which makes setting up a DB plan more expensive than most other options. If you have employees, you're required to make a fixed contribution to their plans, too. But a DB plan can be designed to exclude staff who are under the age of twenty-one or who work part-time (fewer than one thousand hours a year).

Profit-sharing plan

If you're looking for a way to attract and motivate employees, a profit-sharing plan might be a nice option. As the name suggests, you slice off a portion of the company's pretax profits and divvy it up among yourself and your employees. You can contribute up to 25 percent of total payroll compensation (or 20 percent of self-employment income) subject to a $49,000 ceiling. Profit-sharing plans allow you to vary the percentage you contribute from year to year, so you can share the wealth when business is robust or pull back when it's lean.

For more on retirement plan basics, consult the SBA's online guide at www.sba.gov/services/training/nationwide or the NFIB's guide at www.nfib.com/page/retirementTax.html. You might also read *The Wall Street Journal Complete Retirement Guidebook,* which provides tips on calculating your nest egg's ideal size, time lines for making decisions, and advice on investing wisely.

CHAPTER 16

EXIT STRATEGIES

tart-up entrepreneurs seeking angel funding or venture capital aren't the only ones who need to have exit strategies in place. If you've built a successful business, there's one last thing you need to plan: when—and how—to bow out.

Many entrepreneurs dream of leaving the business they created to their offspring. Indeed, about 90 percent of U.S. businesses are family-owned or -controlled, according to the SBA. Others want to sell the business to a new owner and use the proceeds to fund their retirement, launch a new entrepreneurial venture or simply move on to the next chapter in their lives.

Whatever the case, it's critical to map out a smooth transition. In this chapter, we'll take a look at how a 160-year-old family business has perfected the art of handing over the reins to the next generation. We'll also take a look at how to ready your business for the auction block, if that's the better choice for you. You'll need to consider putting a price on the value of your company, timing the sale, structuring the deal, reducing taxes, limiting the legal risks and preparing staff for the transition. All of that takes time and planning, which is why you need to be thinking about your exit strategies many years in advance.

RESOURCES FOR FAMILY-OWNED BUSINESSES

Institute for Family-Owned Business

http://fambusiness.org

This Portland, Maine, nonprofit provides programs and services for family-owned businesses.

Family Business Institute

www.familybusinessinstitute.com

Based in Raleigh, North Carolina, the Family Business Institute offers comprehensive counseling for closely held companies.

Institute for Family Business

www.baylor.edu/business/entrepreneur/family_business

The institute was established in 1987 at Baylor University to disseminate information about family businesses, with the goal of helping these companies survive to the second and third generations.

PASSING THE TORCH

If you're thinking about transferring ownership to your heirs, here is something to consider: only about one-third of family businesses survive the transition to first- or second-generation ownership, according to the Family Firm Institute of Boston. The most common reason for failure? Lack of succession planning on the part of the owner.

Many business owners don't plan for their own succession because, quite simply, they don't want to think about retiring, dying or stepping away from work that's been synonymous with life. Not to mention that planning who will take over your company can be a complicated process. You have to decide which family member (or members) is best for that role, which can cause disagreements and hurt feelings. Some companies choose to stay family-controlled but pick a non–family member to manage the day-to-day operations. (See the box "How Do I Pick a Successor?" on page 171.) You'll also need to consider your estate plan, as the bulk of your net worth is likely tied up in the business. (See the box "Special Estate Planning Needs" on page 172.) For that, it's important to get advice from an attorney who understands family businesses and the transfer of ownership to the next generation. Last, you'll need to communicate your choice of a successor to clients, vendors, suppliers, investors and—especially—employees. The longer all parties involved have to grow accustomed to the idea of a new boss, the better.

A CASE STUDY: HUBBARD-HALL

One of my favorite family business stories is that of Hubbard-Hall, a chemical distributor in Waterbury, Connecticut, which has been family-owned and -operated since 1849. (To put that in perspective, eighteen-wheelers have replaced the horse-drawn carriages used at the time of the company's inception.) This is a company that knows a thing or two about succession, having successfully passed control down through five generations.

Current chairman Chuck Kellogg, seventy-seven, who took over from his father, is now planning the next handoff. And what makes this story especially interesting is that daughter Molly, forty-three, will be the sixth generation—and the first woman—to run the family business.

Both Chuck and Molly had to overcome a few hurdles in preparing for the transition. Chuck comes from a long line of hard workers who don't easily step away from the business, even when they know they should. The running gag is that his father literally never stopped working: one day he went to lunch and never came back. So now, long past retirement age, Chuck is still very much involved in the business. And for her part, Molly, like many children of business owners, needed a way to satisfy her independent streak. Rather than get involved with Hubbard-Hall immediately after college, she attended business school to beef up her credentials. She decided to join the company in the mid-1990s when a position with more autonomy—running a Hubbard-Hall division near Boston, a two-hour drive from corporate headquarters, where her dad worked—became available.

Molly has a sister and two brothers but was the only one of Chuck's children with the professional skills, experience and interest to take over the company. Still, he was hesitant to name her as successor, for reasons unrelated to her business abilities. Molly recalls the company's sesquicentennial celebration in 1999, shortly after she became engaged, when her father gave a big speech, announcing that the business could pass "from father to son-in-law" now that she was getting married. Molly remembers feeling aghast when he said that publicly, especially since she'd been working in the business for many years and thought it was clear that she'd be taking over.

As the story illustrates, the succession planning process is full of challenges, even for a company that's done it as long and as successfully as Hubbard-Hall has. In this case, Chuck Kellogg—who admits to having some old-fashioned views, despite his pride in Molly's accomplishments—had to overcome both his reluctance to leave and his concerns about letting a woman take over what had long been a male-dominated firm.

Still, with time, planning and lots of communication, they were able to overcome these challenges. Over the past ten years, Molly has proven herself to her dad, now joining him in monthly business strategy sessions run by Vistage International, a peer-to-peer membership organization for CEOs. For his part, Chuck has begun stepping away from managing day-to-day operations (assigning others, including Molly's cousin Andrew, to more senior roles) as he inches toward full retirement. In June 2007, he promoted Molly to executive vice president to signal that she would be his successor, and began communicating that fact to staff, customers and others in the industry. In September of that year, Molly took on a new leadership role, kicking off an

HOW DO I PICK A SUCCESSOR?

Finding someone to fill your shoes isn't easy. You'll need to identify a new leader who cares for the company as much as you do. And you'll also need to make sure your decision doesn't ruffle feathers or wreck family relationships. Communication is key, experts say. Here are some tips when choosing your company's next leader:

- Plan a multiday family retreat to discuss the need for a successor and to allow individual family members to express their desires to lead the company. To avoid distraction, schedule the retreat away from the office. Invite all family members, including in-laws.

- If there isn't a clear successor, or more than one family member may be interested in the top spot, write a job description to take some of the emotion out of the decision-making process. Outline what the job requires in terms of skills, work experience and personality.

- If family members want to be owners but not managers, consider a non-family CEO. Ideally, your business will already have top-notch talent who understand the family's values and can be groomed to lead the company. If not, consider using the services of an executive search firm.

- Solicit advice from an outside board of directors, if you have one, or from professionals or consultants familiar with family businesses and succession planning.

ongoing project to grow the company over the next twenty years—a role that helps demonstrate to all that she has a long-term commitment to Hubbard-Hall.

As for that initial hesitancy to pass the business to a woman, Chuck now says his father and grandfather would be "tickled pink" that Molly will be running the family business. Molly says she's able to call her dad on "that part of his brain that is still stuck in the fifties," and they are able to laugh about it. Over

SPECIAL ESTATE PLANNING NEEDS

If you've built a profitable family business that you wish to leave to the next generation, you'll need special estate planning advice, which involves a mix of legal, financial and insurance planning strategies.

Every family business, of course, will have different needs. Your estate planning attorney might suggest, for instance, that you form a family partnership or limited liability company, which would allow you to maintain control while gradually transferring interests to your children. You'll need to figure out how to treat everyone fairly, since a good deal of your estate's worth is likely to be tied up in your company, especially if you've got some family members who wish to operate the business and others who don't. Because of the complexity, it's wise to plan far in advance to avoid conflict and reduce estate and gift taxes.

time, much of Chuck's concern has faded as she's grown into the senior management position.

Molly, who has three young daughters and a son, realizes she'll need to come up with her own exit strategy down the road. She hopes one of her children will have an interest in the family business. "I want to grow it, give the people who work for Hubbard-Hall a nice lifestyle and pass it on to the next generation," she says. "I feel very much like a steward. I've been given a very great and special gift, and it's my obligation to pass it on."

SELLING THE BUSINESS

Passing the business along to the next generation might not be part of your plan. Instead, it may be time to take what you've built with blood, sweat and tears—and cash out.

Selling a business is a lot like sprucing up your house for sale: you'll want to make sure everything is neat, orderly and presented in the best light possible for maximum dollar. And much the way a home owner might use the services of a real estate agent, you'll likely want to enlist the services of a business broker or a merger-and-acquisition specialist.

That's because unless you have started and sold many businesses, you likely are not familiar enough with the ins and outs of the process. You'll want to make sure you deal with an expert who is well schooled in assigning a value, structuring a sale in the most tax-friendly manner and negotiating the best price, especially if there are multiple potential buyers. As a rule of thumb, businesses that post less than $1 million in annual revenues typically use a business broker; multimillion-dollar businesses often use the services of a merger-and-acquisition specialist. Ask your lawyer, banker, accountant or other business owners for a referral; sites such as BizBuySell.com provide more information on the process.

To find out what's it like to sell a company, I spoke with Barry Evans, owner of Acquisition Services Group, a La Jolla, California, merger-and-acquisition firm that assists individuals who want to sell privately owned companies with market values between $1 million and $20 million. He spelled out the documents that you'll need to prepare a valuation of your company, which is the first step in selling your company.

- Tax returns from the past five years

- Internal financial statements from the past five years

- Year-to-date financial information

- Year-to-date financial information for the year-ago period

- Minutes of board meetings and annual meetings (if a corporation)

Those documents, of course, are just the start, Evans says. Most businesses will need to adjust financial statements to better reflect actual earning power—a process called recasting, which is widely accepted in the industry. Essentially, while operating the company, you may have employed tactics—such as giving yourself perks, putting family members on the payroll, or steering profits into capital improvements—designed to keep the company's profits low, for tax purposes. When you recast, you add those expenses back in to present a picture of the company's normal operation.

Another piece of the valuation is an analysis of risk. For instance, a company that relies heavily on one big customer for the bulk of its revenues would be considered high-risk, while a business that has hundreds of customers, a long-term lease and noncompete agreements already in place with its employees would be lower risk.

Once you've got a valuation, there's more work to be done, according to Evans. Essentially, you'll need to disclose the nitty-gritty details of your business in a selling memorandum that would be confidentially marketed to potential buyers. Some typical information it might contain:

- A history of when you started the business, hired employees and (if applicable) secured patents

- A roster of employees (including yourself) outlining job descriptions, levels of experience, salaries and whether they are unionized

- A description of your customer base, detailing customers' size, location and the amount of business you conduct with them

- A review of your location, such as whether you own or lease the space (If it's a lease, indicate if it's assumable by a new owner.)

- A listing of all owned or leased equipment, trucks or trailers, with a description of their condition

A special note: you'll also want to disclose any litigation or regulatory hurdles you've dealt with in past years—and any other negatives that may become a headache for the new owner. By disclosing that information, you'll help protect yourself from a lawsuit down the road, Evans says. You'll also want to outline any improvements that the new business owner might make to the business.

Keep in mind that readying your business for sale requires far more than preparing financial statements and getting your documents in order. You may need to renegotiate lease, vendor and employee agreements and pay all back taxes or other outstanding debt.

And in a tough economy, you'll want to take steps to maximize revenues and minimize operating expenses, Evans says. After all, it's your profits that will undoubtedly attract buyers to your business. That might require some cutbacks, such as trimming staff if need be. You may also need to tighten up any operating problems, such as investigating why inventory routinely goes lost or missing. And you might want to reexamine your credit-granting procedures, especially if you're worried about customers missing payments.

Once you've got your business's financial and operational houses in order, your broker or specialist should actively market that information to potential buyers. (Potential buyers, who may be competitors, should be required to sign a confidentiality agreement before reviewing the information.) You'll also want to keep mum about your plans to employees, vendors and customers, all of whom might take flight upon learning that you wish to sell the business. Ideally, you'll inform them of your plan to leave when you're announcing the new owner, says Evans. Often, a business owner will stay on for a period of time as a consultant during the transition process.

In the best of circumstances, you'll get offers from numerous buyers—and a critical next step will be deciding how to structure the deal in the most tax-advantaged way possible. Most small businesses are sold through either a stock sale or an asset sale, and there are various tax consequences depending on your company's legal entity, your personal investment and other factors. If your company is valued at $1 million, you might end up with after-tax proceeds in the range of $450,000 to $850,000, depending on those variables, according to Evans. To ensure the most profits, he says, plan the sale far in advance so you can eke out as much tax savings as possible.

PART THREE

BALANCING WORK AND LIFE

CHAPTER 17

MANAGING STRESS

Running a business isn't easy. Work-related pressure can lead to a host of stress-induced problems: headaches, sleepless nights, irritability, weight gain and lost productivity, among others.

Business owners often cite the following as their most common sources of stress:

- Excessive workloads

- Concerns about making enough money

- Fears (when employees are involved) about making payroll

- Underperforming when it comes to meeting customers' expectations

- Feeling increased pressure to succeed when many things (such as personal savings, a corporate career and time away from family) have been sacrificed

The statistics on survival only underscore the stress placed on small business owners. About one-third of new businesses don't make it past two years, and almost 60 percent fold within four years, according to the Small Business Administration's Office of Advocacy. Causes of failure range from lack of capital to inexperience.

The life of a small business owner is tough for sure. But if you're reading this book, you're already on the right track toward a less stressful life and more successful business. You'll learn that the smartest way to achieve both is by planning ahead.

GIVE YOURSELF DIRECTION

It's clear from numerous interviews of entrepreneurs that the best method of combating business-related stress is to plan. Entrepreneurs who haven't updated or assembled their business plan (for more on business plans, see Chapter 2) can feel directionless, inefficient and overwhelmed—all of which contribute to stress. Writing out even a simple plan can prevent overload while also providing a viable road map to success.

Too many business owners make the mistake of working *in* the business and not *on* it. While it's easy to get caught up in the daily grind, you'll ultimately reduce your stress by taking a step back to focus on your business in the long-term scheme of things. Essentially, you want to anticipate everything that might happen, and everything that's in your control to make happen. The best time to do that is often during quiet periods, or, as some business owners prefer, on a mini-retreat away from the office. During this time, your goal is to take a look at how the business has been performing—what's worked, what hasn't—and to come up with a plan for the year ahead. If you need more clients, target specific areas where you think you can drum up business. Come up with a marketing plan. Develop a budget by figuring out how much you need to set aside for quarterly tax payments, capital expenditures, your retirement plan, employee salaries and other areas. All of this advance planning will allow you to spend less time putting out fires and more time meeting the business goals you've outlined. As a

THE BENEFITS OF A COMPANY RETREAT

Barbara Bickham, founder of the consulting firm TechGenii in Los Angeles, takes a company retreat twice a year to Hawaii's Kona Coast. A solo entrepreneur, Bickham invites clients and business associates along on the midyear retreat (usually in June) and has discovered that diving, golfing and hiking among the petroglyph rock carvings is an excellent way to relieve stress while cultivating work relationships.

At the end of the year, Bickham returns by herself to spend time reviewing the company's performance while also taking walks along the beach, getting lava-rock massages and climbing volcanos. "I'm in a relaxed area and in a place I love, and I'm rejuvenating myself," she says. She'll often ask herself questions such as "How do I get more clients? How do I close more sales? What type of marketing activities should I do?" while jotting down ideas in a notebook or laptop. "I'm in a place where I don't have to take a call and I don't have to read the BlackBerry," she says. "It helps me get perspective."

result, you will feel more in control and less vulnerable to stress.

WHEN STRESS HAPPENS

Of course, even with the most solid business plan, most entrepreneurs can't eliminate stress. Many business owners also suffer profoundly from work-related tension when they neglect to carve out time for their personal lives. Luckily, there are smart ways you can relieve some of this stress.

TAKE MENTAL HEALTH TIME

Finding an escape from managing cash flow, finishing jobs or dealing with disgruntled customers is tough for business owners, who often work on weekends and forget to take vacations.

Some entrepreneurs have come up with innovative ways to ensure they leave the office behind, if only for a few hours. Three nights a week, Frances Black, founder of New York illustration agency Arts Counsel, straps on a pair of high heels and practices the waltz, mambo and hustle with her longtime dance partner. She loves dancing because of the intense concentration needed; she's forced to focus on her footwork rather than her business. Finding a creative outlet through hobbies such as dancing, painting or collecting can stave off the hallmarks of chronic stress: illness and mental fatigue. Taking short breaks to read a book, listen to music or walk in the park also helps reduce stress.

Make Fitness a Priority

A regular workout regimen often falls by the wayside when a person starts a business. Numerous studies show that exercise relieves stress, boosts creativity and improves self-esteem. Yet many entrepreneurs say it's hard to justify taking time for fitness when they could be selling, marketing or otherwise growing the business. The best way to get the exercise you need is to schedule workout time on the calendar, just like any important business meeting. A business owner who leases office space might want to make sure that location is near a gym, has space for a workout room, or even has showers to allow biking or running to work. Consider hiring the services of a personal trainer; the financial commitment might make you think twice about skipping appointments.

Eat Right

In a 2007 study, the American Psychological Association found that 43 percent of stressed-out people deal with their frustrations by overeating or munching on junk foods. Some business owners battle the bulge by making sure their offices are stocked with healthy foods. Whether you're based at home or at an office, keep a drawer of healthy snacks (such as dried fruits, nuts, granola bars or dark chocolate) and a mini-refrigerator stocked with fresh items (baby carrots, hummus, cottage cheese or yogurt) to avoid turning to candy bars and chips when stress strikes.

GET YOUR REST

In the start-up phase, a business owner can lose more than seven hundred hours of sleep a year—similar to the amount a parent loses in the first year of a newborn's life, according to James B. Maas, a sleep expert at Cornell University. While you can get by for a while, sleep deprivation eventually hampers performance, ruins a person's ability to multitask and contributes to an array of health problems. If stress about the business routinely keeps you up at night, allow yourself a short period of "worry time" prior to bed. Jot down everything you need to accomplish the next day, then let it go. Then spend at least a half hour relaxing in some manner, such as reading or meditation. And if you don't get enough sleep, take a short nap the next day. Research by NASA has shown that a twenty-six-minute nap increased pilots' performance by 34 percent. It's called the power nap for a reason!

CHAPTER 18

THE END OF PAID LEAVE

Here's a secret about owning your own business: you'll never take a vacation or a sick day without worrying again. What are most business owners concerned about? These are the big trouble spots, according to a number of studies:

- Losing an important client

- Missing an opportunity to make money

- Equipment breaking down

- Staff making bad judgment calls in your absence

So how can you manage to miss work from time to time without losing your business in the process? This chapter will show you the way.

NO MORE VACATION DAYS

Despite all the worries you might have about taking time off, research indicates that taking a true vacation (usually defined as long, uninterrupted moments of relaxation) is one of the most important things a business owner can do to stay fresh, motivated and sharp when it comes to decision making.

It's easier said than done. One business owner told me she felt like a "flake" taking a breather, especially when her public relations business wasn't established and running as smoothly as she wanted. That feeling of guilt or irresponsibility might be something that corporate workaholics experience, too, but it's magnified when you're the business owner. In fact, most entrepreneurs say they aren't comfortable taking a vacation for the first two or three years of the start-up's life—if ever.

Especially in the early years, when resources are limited, you'll likely do pretty much everything yourself, from sales and marketing to tax preparation and accounting. If you take a vacation, there's a feeling that nothing work related will get done in your absence.

Even if you have employees to cover for you, you're likely to spend most of your time off worrying that they can't handle it. And then there are the business owners who try to take a vacation but usually end up doing so much work on it that they're not sure they actually got away. For example, take Bonnie Harris, founder of Wax Marketing in St. Paul, Minnesota. An avid skier, Harris installed a special headset in her ski helmet so that she can take work calls while on the slopes. One year, she even booked a client on a national TV show while riding the chairlift.

Remember, one of the goals in creating a successful business is to let it run on its own. To use the parenting analogy again, it's similar to having a child: you want that toddler or teenager to grow into an adult who is capable of surviving without you. So if you're one of those business owners who swears up and down that he or she can't relax on vacation without constantly checking in, get over yourself.

Also, if you have employees, not taking a vacation or frequently checking in while away can create an unpleasant work environment. You're not-so-subtly sending the message that vacation isn't encouraged at your workplace and that you don't trust your staff to handle work in your absence. Neither is good for employee morale.

Regardless of whether you have employees, all business owners need to get away every once in a while. You may still worry some while trying to kick the habit, but you can make it easier on yourself if you use the following strategies.

ALERT CLIENTS AND CUSTOMERS WELL IN ADVANCE

Many business owners worry that they'll reveal themselves to be a small operation if they take a vacation. In reality, your clients and customers likely do business with you because you're not a faceless corporation, and most people understand and respect your need for R&R. The key is to give plenty of notice. Make calls or send e-mails alerting your clients that you'll be on vacation (and provide the specific dates) a few weeks in advance. That way, they can ask you questions, get updates on projects, buy services or schedule appointments before you leave. Make sure to provide clients and customers with the contact information of staff who will be handling operations in your absence. Solo entrepreneurs often give important clients or customers a cell phone number where they can be reached in case of emergency.

DELEGATE RESPONSIBILITIES TO TRUSTED STAFF

Train employees to handle projects—and problems—in your absence. Before you leave, walk them through the assigned tasks and supply them with useful information about the clients, customers, vendors, suppliers or distributors they'll be dealing with.

If you don't have employees, consider a reliable virtual assistant, an independent contractor who works from his or her own home (hence the term *virtual*) and can handle an array of administrative or technical duties, such as checking e-mail or voice-mail, setting or canceling appointments, entering sales leads into a database, or updating websites. (For help finding a VA, visit the International Virtual Assistants Association at www.ivaa.org.)

WRITE DOWN ALL YOUR POLICIES AND PROCEDURES

As discussed in Chapter 10, most entrepreneurs will develop specific polices and procedures over time for everything from handling incoming calls to taking Web orders. If you don't have a manual for how your business operates, it's difficult for anyone to step in and run it in your absence. By getting your company's practices out of your head and onto paper (or, more likely, an electronic document), you make it easier for employees or assistants to pick up where you left off.

TACK VACATION ONTO A WORK TRIP

It may not be as relaxing as a proper getaway, but many business owners save time and money by linking vacation to business travel. For starters, adding an extra day or two to a business trip for personal pursuits—whether that's a massage or a round of golf—is a more efficient, effective way to take a breather without worrying too much about losing business. It's also a cheaper way to take a vacation: as long as the primary purpose is business and the cost isn't overly extravagant, you can deduct many of the travel costs on your taxes.

Alicia Rockmore, who travels several times a month for her organizational products company, Buttoned Up, based in Ann Arbor, Michigan, says the last thing she feels like doing when she gets home from a business trip is getting on an airplane for fun. So she'll often tack extra time onto a business trip for recreation, such as going to a spa or visiting friends. On trips to Orlando, she'll bring her young daughter and a nanny, scheduling outings to Disney World in the mornings and work meetings in the afternoons or evenings.

Although combining vacation with work travel might not be as indulgent as a truly separate trip, it's certainly better than no respite at all when your leisure time is limited. You might remind family members of this fact if they're complaining about your switching back into work mode while they're still in vacation mode.

HAVE PINCH HITTERS FILL IN

This doesn't work for every industry, but business owners such as psychologists, personal trainers and public relations professionals can form a network of professionals who can fill in as needed. In some cases, temporary help trained in your field can assist. Look to industry groups to find like-minded associates. For instance, the Professional Association of Innkeepers International in Haddon Heights, New Jersey, trains interested parties to be "interim innkeepers" who can step in and tend to your B&B while you seek out some R&R of your own.

TAKE VACATION DURING THE SLOW PERIODS

Many business owners find that the traditionally quiet time between Christmas and the new year is an opportune time to take a breather. Often, clients or customers are taking those same days off as well, so there are fewer interruptions and less of a need to check e-mails or phone messages. Some entrepreneurs shut the office down completely, giving employees those days off, too. Companies that can't shut down completely sometimes operate with a skeleton staff (business owners can compensate employees who work over the holidays with extra money or vacation days).

For entrepreneurs who run retail shops or seasonal enterprises, on the other hand, the holidays can be the busiest time of year. For them, the best time to take a vacation might be a slow period during January or the summer months.

A WIRED VACATION?

Technology has made it easier for business owners to take the office wherever they go. Cell phones, laptop computers and wireless devices allow many entrepreneurs to strike a compromise: they can get away but still be on call as needed.

But here's the problem: constantly checking your Black-Berry and taking work-related calls while on the beach or the ski slopes ruins many a relaxing moment and causes friction with loved ones. Here are some smart ways to use technology, without ruining everyone's fun:

- Set aside specific times of the day (such as once in the morning and then once in the evening) to check, and honor those. Parents of young children, for instance, often get up before the kids are awake, to tend to work matters. Above all, resist the urge to frequently read e-mails or make work calls.

- Stick to the basics. Leave the fancy headsets or videoconferencing technologies at home. By limiting the number of work-related gadgets you bring, you effectively limit how much work you can do.

- Before you leave home, make sure the devices you do bring are working. Don't waste time on vacation fiddling with a faulty laptop or signalless cell phone. Check hotels ahead of time to see if they provide high-speed Internet connections. Bring adapters as needed for overseas travel.

Accept the Fact That You'll Lose Money

As mentioned, one of the top reasons that entrepreneurs have trouble taking vacation is that they worry they'll miss an opportunity to make money. Chances are you will. It's best to accept that and move on, says Robin Ryan, a career counselor in Seattle, Washington. "It's the cost of having your own business and not enough people to run it because it's so small," she says. "It's a necessary loss." Ryan recommends that business owners take two weeks off a year to experience a true detachment from work—and console themselves on lost opportunities and money with the fact that this time off is potentially raising their own productivity and energy levels on return, saving them from burnout.

DEALING WITH ILLNESS WITHOUT SICK DAYS

It's a fact of life—you'll get sick, or your kids will get sick. And then the big question arises: What happens to all the work you've got to get done?

Dealing with illness can be one of the toughest challenges a small business owner has to face. Whether it's a twenty-four-hour bug or a more serious condition, such as cancer, a herniated disc or Lyme disease, having a plan for when sickness strikes is critical.

Insurance can cover the cost of medical treatment or reimburse you for the period your business was interrupted. But in the meantime, failing to deliver on customer commitments can spell disaster for your small company. Many business owners who have dealt with illness tell us one central notion guided their actions: keep the business open.

At the age of thirty-eight, Terri Hornsby was sitting in the Houston office of her promotional products company, TLC Adcentives, when she got a call from her doctor's office. The lump she had discovered was indeed breast cancer. Her first reaction? Understandably, to cry. Her second reaction? To focus on saving not just her life but that of her three-year-old business.

Hornsby immediately stepped out of her office and came up with a plan. She appointed her assistant (who happens to be her sister) as second in command, in charge of processing all orders, handling invoices and researching quotes for clients.

Then, knowing she'd need surgery, Hornsby called up her support network (mostly friends she'd met through women's groups and her church) and asked them for help; in the weeks that followed, they cooked for her, picked up her son from day care, and even cleaned her house. That gave Hornsby more energy to devote to the business. She often juggled chemotherapy sessions with client visits, talking to clients over the phone on days she felt particularly weak. After a grueling eight months, Hornsby's cancer was gone but her business was thriving.

I hope you never have to deal with a sickness as serious as cancer, but even something as minor as a cold can mean lost opportunities for small business owners. So it's essential to have plans in place for illnesses large or small.

Entrepreneurs say dealing with sickness often entails a lot of muddling through mixed with other strategies. Here are some tips for keeping your business healthy, even when you're not.

Don't Be Indispensable

Often, the owner is so integral to the operations of a small enterprise that when he or she is waylaid by an extended illness, things fall apart. An indispensable owner can be one of a company's greatest vulnerabilities.

Develop a family member, key employee or management team member into a reliable interim leader in the event you are incapacitated. Introduce that person to valued clients or customers so that they will be comfortable working with him or her in your absence. If you're a solo entrepreneur, look into creating a network of trusted business associates in the same field who can cover for you if an emergency situation arises (establish an hourly rate, if need be).

As a business owner, you also need to worry about what happens if employees get sick and can't perform the tasks they are scheduled to complete. Some companies make sure that each employee has a "point person" to cover for him or her in the event of illness. At some businesses, workers share jobs and can easily step in if need be. (For more on employee sick days, see the box on page 194.)

GET ORGANIZED

In the event you need to delegate, the process will be easier if you have compiled contact information for clients, suppliers and vendors, plus made a list of upcoming appointments, projects or assignments. Make it a habit, at the end of the day or week, to at least make a mental checklist of tasks that need to be accomplished in the short term. That way, if you're unexpectedly sick, you can easily assign tasks to your second in command or interim help.

BE PROACTIVE

If you're, say, the parent of a preschooler, there's not much you can do to prevent the occasional germ or bug from invading your house. But there are some ailments that you can ward off simply by adjusting your lifestyle. For some business owners, that means giving up competitive sports likely to cause injury, such as weekend soccer leagues or pickup basketball. For others, it's sticking to healthier habits, including eating right, getting plenty of sleep, quitting smoking, and drinking in moderation. Still others say they regularly practice yoga or Pilates to stay fit.

One of the more difficult practices for entrepreneurs to break is working to the extreme, which can result in burnout, chronic fatigue, weight gain, heart disease and a host of other ailments. Many entrepreneurs combat tendencies to overwork by sticking to strict rules, such as limiting work to certain hours, taking vacations, scheduling time for hobbies and turning off wireless e-mail devices on the weekend.

DO YOU PROVIDE PAID SICK DAYS FOR EMPLOYEES?

If you've got employees, chances are they'll call in sick from time to time. That's why it's important to develop a sick-leave policy.

In some areas of the country—most notably San Francisco—small business owners don't have a choice: they must provide paid sick leave to employees. Business owners elsewhere can provide paid sick days at their own discretion.

What you offer depends on what you can afford, although many owners decide that paid sick leave is simply a good business practice. The easiest approach is to decide how many sick days an employee should get per year (make it consistent for all employees, to avoid discrimination claims). Then put the policy in writing and make sure employees get a copy when they're hired.

The Family and Medical Leave Act, the federal law that grants twelve workweeks of unpaid, protected leave for specific medical conditions, applies to businesses with fifty or more employees. The National Federation for Independent Business, which has protested government-mandated sick leave, says its research shows that small businesses grant virtually all requests for family and medical leave.

CHAPTER 19

WORKING FROM HOME (OR, LIVING IN YOUR OFFICE)

Y ou have to put your business somewhere, and for many people, that location is the extra bedroom, dining room table or spare corner in the garage.

About 52 percent of all small businesses are home based, representing a broad swath of industries from software development and mail-order sales to plumbing and general contracting, according to statistics from the SBA's Office of Advocacy. That number has grown in recent years as technology (and general acceptance) has made it easier to work from home.

For many start-ups, a home office is the natural choice. Corporate employees with entrepreneurial visions sometimes open a "business on the side" out of their homes. Newbie business owners with big dreams but limited resources frequently start the business at home to test out ideas and save on the costs of renting a space.

In some cases, the home can serve as an incubator for a business that eventually requires a separate physical location. Other times, the venture is well suited to be run out of one's home permanently, such as a bed-and-breakfast, a child care facility, or any number of professional services businesses (think accounting, consulting or marketing) that require only a small office. And in a tough economy or down period, a business owner who has rented office space might return to a home office as a way to trim overhead costs.

What are the advantages of working from home? Home-based entrepreneurs list the following:

- No commute. This saves not only time but money related to gas, car maintenance or public transportation tickets.

- Flexibility. Not only can you set your own hours, but you have the ability to throw in laundry or walk the dog at will.

- No dress code, unless you need to meet with clients or customers.

- Tax write-offs. (See "Do I Get a Tax Break or What?" on page 200.)

- More time with children. Even those who employ a child care worker say they can stop work to have lunch with kids, take breaks in the playground or just be there when needed.

Yet there are some distinct disadvantages to working from home, too. Most frequently cited is the lack of social interaction, especially for people who live by themselves. For instance, Jeff Louderback, a home-based publicist in Orlando, Florida, starts each day by shaving, dressing professionally and then heading to the office, which happens to be the spare bedroom in his two-bedroom condo. Sometimes he takes his laptop to a local café just so he can be around other people. "I'm a very social, talkative person, so sometimes I do get really lonely," he says.

For others, the home is one giant distraction. A pile of dirty dishes, a screaming child or even a sunny patio might compete for attention over a tedious work project. Often, friends and family who don't understand you are truly working might call, stop by or otherwise interrupt your work routine.

The home can be a difficult place to meet customers or clients, especially if you don't have an extra room or an appropriate place to host a business meeting. Despite the growing number of home-based businesses, there's still an unfortunate stigma associated with working from home versus a professional office. (Many business owners compensate for this by using a post office box instead of a home address, designing a high-quality website, using professional stationery, keeping a dedicated business phone line and hosting meetings at a coffeehouse or restaurant.)

When it comes to hiring employees, some home-based entrepreneurs say there isn't enough space or that it feels too invasive to their privacy to have their staff in the house. The majority of home-based businesses (about 93 percent) don't have employees, according to SBA statistics. Those home-based businesses that do typically only have one to four employees, and often it's the need to hire employees that forces many home-based entrepreneurs to rent space elsewhere.

Last, the line between work and personal life can easily blur when working from home. There might be stacks of documents on the kitchen table, piles of marketing products in the bedroom or children running in and out of your work space. As such, it's important to come up with a set of rules and practices to maintain some degree of separation between your work and personal life when they are sharing the same physical space. Here are some ways to do that:

Have a separate space for your office.

Most ideally, your work space is in a separate room, with a door that closes, with good ventilation and lighting. Work-life balance experts agree that the bedroom is the worst place for a home office, as work becomes the first and last thing you see each day. A home office can be tricky in a small apartment, but screens or cabinets can help physically separate your work and living spaces when you don't have a spare room.

Install office equipment.

Make sure you have a phone line and a computer (with high-speed Internet access) that are dedicated to your business. That way you separate work and personal calls, and you don't have to share your computer with other members of the household who might want to use it to check e-mail, surf the Web, and so on. Also, it's helpful at the end of the workday or on the weekend to have a computer not associated with work to use for personal pursuits, such as messaging or shopping. Make sure to install any necessary business software on your work computer, and consider other office-grade equipment as needed: copiers, scanners, fax, work desks, filing cabinets and the like.

Set a timetable.

It's tempting to work whenever you please. But keeping regular business hours (such as 8:00 a.m.–5:00 p.m., Monday through Friday, with weekends off) will assist you in dealing with clients, customers, suppliers and vendors—and make it easier for you to have a social life. Some home-based entrepreneurs fashion their hours around logical periods of productivity, such as when a spouse leaves for work or kids go off to school. It's important for single home-based entrepreneurs to have a finite end of the day (which for others might be when the spouse or kids come home). One way to end the day might be to head to the gym; a regular fitness routine is not only good for physical and mental health but also an effective way to get out of work mode.

Take breaks.

A big challenge for home-based business owners, especially those used to working in office environments, is to set aside time during the day for small breathers or even lunch. The responsibility falls on the home-based entrepreneur to carve out those times during the day to put work down or turn away from the computer. Short breaks can reduce stress, improve productivity and prevent burnout. For those who miss social interactions, lunch can be an opportune time to meet with friends or colleagues over a meal.

Limit household tasks.

While it's great to be able to throw in a load of laundry or vacuum the carpet, household tasks can be distracting. Be disciplined about not letting household errands interfere with your work day. Consider getting a housekeeper to free up more of your time and energy for work.

Get child care.

While many parents choose to be home based to be closer to their kids, young ones can easily distract you from work, making it difficult to concentrate on a project or talk on the phone. Consider getting full- or part-time child care help, or sharing child care responsibilities with a spouse or family members. For more on parenting while working from home, see Chapter 20.

Communicate to others that you are really working.

Make sure those close to you respect your decision to work at home. Ask friends and family not to call or stop by during the day, or if they do, to keep it brief. Chris Russell, founder of the job-posting site AllCountyJobs.com in Trumbull, Connecticut, says even his wife, who works outside the home, sometimes forgets that he's trying to work. "My wife will say to me, 'Can you go to the dry cleaners for me? Can you start dinner early?'" he says. "I give her a little friendly reminder: 'I'm working, dear.'"

DO I GET A TAX BREAK OR WHAT?

Much as you might have trouble separating work and personal matters, the IRS has difficulties with this, too. But it's worth jumping through the seemingly endless hoops required to get a tax deduction for your home office if you qualify.

First, you must use a portion of your home exclusively and regularly for business. It's the "exclusive" part that typically trips people up. That means, essentially, that your work space can't double as a guest bedroom, playroom or recreational den. What best meets the IRS's approval? An office with a separate door, although even a section of a room that is off-limits to personal activities would work.

Next, your home office must be the principal place where you conduct business. That means your home is the place where you regularly deal with clients, customers or patients. Say you're a consultant with office space available elsewhere; then you probably don't qualify. There is an exception, though, for people who make their living in the field, such as self-employed sales representative, contractors, plumbers, veterinarians and the like. If that's the case and you use your home office for administrative and management activities, then it likely qualifies as your principal place of business.

If these two conditions are met, then deductible expenses include a percentage of your rent or mortgage interest, not to mention utility bills, home repairs, maintenance, real estate taxes and other costs. The portion of your expenses that you can deduct is based on the percentage of your home used for business.

Because the home office deduction is frequently abused, the IRS keeps a close eye on those who claim one. Careful records, plus photos of your home office space, can come in handy in the event of an audit. There are also some possible negative tax consequences: you may have to pay a capital gains tax on the depreciation you've taken if you one day sell your home, provided your home has increased in value.

You'll also need to be prepared for a time-draining tax form. To claim a home office deduction, you must fill out Form 8829, which, depending on the year, is over forty lines long and contains the words "see instructions" numerous times.

Give yourself time to get it right.

Starting or transitioning to a home office might not be easy at first. Give yourself time to come up with a routine, make some rules and figure out what works and what doesn't.

ADDITIONAL RESOURCES

IRS Publication 587, "Business Use of Your Home"
www.irs.gov/pub/irs-pdf/p587.pdf
This pamphlet prepared by the IRS provides information on figuring and claiming the deduction for business use of your home.

Business Owner's Toolkit: Home Office Deduction Calculator
www.toolkit.cch.com/text/p07_2740.asp

CHAPTER 20

JUGGLING THE DEMANDS OF FAMILY AND WORK

For many people, especially home-based entrepreneurs, the decision to start a business has a lot to do with family: running your own company, rather than working for someone else, means more control of your schedule and greater flexibility to tend to the needs of your children. Or so the thinking goes.

In reality, simultaneously juggling the demands of children and a small business can be taxing, leaving entrepreneurs stressed, exhausted and certainly overworked—and often feeling like they have no more time for family than they did in the corporate world. Take Michelle Knoll, who's raising three young sons while running a public relations firm out of her Minneapolis home. Knoll says she gets much of her work accomplished two times of day: the kids' naptime and bedtime. She predicts that in a few years, when the kids are off to school, running the business will seem like the easiest thing she's ever done because she won't have to deal with screaming or "Mom, Mom, Mom" in her ear while she's trying to work. (For more on home-based business owners/parents, see "Parents with Home-Based Businesses" on page 206.)

Many parents who are successfully running a business say it takes careful planning, sometimes driven by desperation, to reach that sweet spot where they feel like they are doing both jobs well. For example, Ben Chestnut, cofounder of Atlanta software company MailChimp.com, was "in a daze" for about six months in 2007 after he found out his wife was expecting. He had no clue how he'd manage his business (located outside the home) and care for a newborn. But he was able to plan and make it work.

How he handled impending parenthood provides a good lesson for other entrepreneurs. First, Chestnut reviewed what he did for the company, and decided to focus on his core strengths—managing operations, planning budgets and marketing—and hand off customer service (his self-described weakness) to a colleague.

Then Chestnut wrote out thorough instructions for the company's project management system so that he could drop everything and leave someone else in charge when his wife went into labor. He adjusted his schedule to start and finish earlier. Following his son's birth, he worked by day at the office and arrived home in early evening to take over the "night shift" from his wife. Now he's found that parenthood has left him with great ambitions: he wants to ramp up sales so he can afford a bigger house. "It's really motivated me," he says.

Many parents who are also business owners say the arrival of a newborn forced them to be more efficient, more reliant on key employees and ultimately more mindful of their personal lives, all good business practices they should have been following anyhow. And certainly the flexibility and autonomy that small business owners wield comes in handy when it comes to adjusting workloads and schedules. Here is some other advice offered by parents (both moms and dads) who have figured out a way to raise a baby while building a business:

Match your hours to your kids' schedules.

It's important (some might say critical) for parents to set firm work hours, especially when they rely on nannies, day care workers or family members to care for their children. Jen Groover, a Philadelphia entrepreneur who launched her Butler Bag purse company when her twin daughters were nine months old, says her entire staff knows that she walks out the door each day at 5:00 p.m. Not only does she need to relieve her au pair, but she wants to spend quality time with the kids in the evening. If she's got more work to finish, sometimes she'll tackle it after the twins have gone to bed at night.

Use technology to spend more time with your children.

Wireless e-mail devices and laptop computers make it easier to be mobile, especially in the early days when the baby is first born. We've interviewed female entrepreneurs who say they were BlackBerrying up into the final stages of labor; male entrepreneurs have told us that it was easier for them to stay home and help their wives because of technology. (Many business owners, however, make it a rule to turn off technology at night or on the weekends so as not to abuse it.)

Let kids help you prioritize.

Perhaps it's some version of nesting, but many business owners say they became more productive, more focused and, in general, more organized at work as they prepared to become parents. As discussed in earlier chapters, one big tip is to get your policies and procedures out of your head and onto paper. That will help you step away from the office and leave others in charge, whether that's for taking a vacation, dealing with illness or caring for a child.

Learn to delegate.

Business owners, by nature, like being in control, so this is a tough one. But the double responsibilities of being a parent and a business owner can be too much for one person to handle. Learn to rely more on key employees or virtual assistants to help manage the business. Share child care duties with hired help or family members. Hire someone to mow the lawn, pick up groceries or clean your house to free up more of your time for family and the business.

PARENTS WITH HOME-BASED BUSINESSES

Parents who are home-based entrepreneurs have another set of hurdles—namely, the fact that they are in the same building as their children. That means the business owner/parent can be easily distracted by a young one crying or needing attention. And the proximity can lead to feelings of guilt. Parents (especially moms) say they feel bad having to close the door and get work done; at the same time, they can feel unprofessional or like a bad businessperson if they're on the phone and a child is crying or talking in the background.

What further complicates the situation for home-based entrepreneurs is the fact that they typically don't have staff or even part-time employees to support them. Here are a few suggestions to help you be a more successful work-at-home mom or dad:

- Figure out a regular work schedule that works for your family and your business. Some parents are able to split child care responsibilities, with, for instance, Mom caring for the child during the day, then handing the baby off to Dad at night so she can work on the business. Make sure your family members and friends know the plan, to prevent interruptions. Keep a daily planner to manage your day and prioritize your tasks.

- Explore your child care options. Consider getting in-home care (at least part-time)—particularly if you have young children who need a lot of attention—or taking kids to day care as needed to give you more time to devote to the business. Have a support network in place, whether that's other work-at-home parents or friends who can provide advice, backup child care or just a sympathetic ear as needed.

- And of course, get work done, but don't shut out kids completely. You don't want your children to think of your business as the thing that takes you away from them. Wally Bock, a home-based consultant in Greensboro, North Carolina, says he used to tell his kids (now grown) not to open his office door unless it required 911. But when they wanted him to attend ball games or recitals, he'd mark it down on his calendar in a grand ceremony and honor their requests.

- It's also possible to let kids into the office during slow periods, when no client calls are scheduled or menial tasks can be performed. Nicola Ries Taggart, who runs her life-coaching business True Insights Coaching out of her Alameda, California, home, keeps a box of crayons in the office so her young daughter can color while Mom gets stuff done at her desk. Other times you might get out of work mode to focus on your kids, eating lunch with them or picking them up from school.

ADDITIONAL RESOURCES

The Home Office Parent by Jennifer Kalita
This guidebook tells how to raise kids and profits under one roof.

Home-Based Working Moms
www.hbwm.com
HBWM, started by Lesley Spencer Pyle so she could spend more time with her children, is a professional association and online community of parents who work from home.

Mompreneurs Online
www.mompreneursonline.com
Patricia Cobe and Ellen H. Parlapiano, the two woman who trademarked the term *mompreneur,* share strategies and successes on this site.

AS A BUSINESS OWNER, CAN I WRITE OFF THE COST OF CHILD CARE?

The answer is no. While many business owners would like to write off the cost of a nanny as a corporate expense, the IRS prohibits this. Why? Because even though you might require child care in order to work, a nanny is still deemed a personal expense, unlike a corporate meal or hotel stay you might write off.

Can you make the nanny an employee of the corporation and get some tax breaks that way? That also doesn't pass muster with the IRS, as the nanny doesn't directly contribute to the success of the company the way other employees would.

One possible option, if the parents work together in the business, is for one spouse to make the other an employee and direct the company to contribute up to $5,000 (free of taxes) to cover the cost of the spouse-employee's dependent care. This option has a few catches—for starters, if you have other employees, you have to offer the same deal to everyone. And the rules vary depending on whether the business is structured as an LLC, an S corporation, a sole proprietorship or a regular corporation. Before setting up such a program, check with your tax advisor to see if it makes sense for your situation.

JOLLY'S JAVA
BUSINESS PLAN

Your written business plan should describe your company, outline your goals and serve as a road map for future activities. To learn more about writing a business plan, check the Small Business Administration's website, which offers a tutorial and the answers to frequently asked questions, and the National Federation of Independent Business's online Small Business Toolbox, which provides tips. Another resource is BPlans.com, which is owned by Palo Alto Software, which offers free sample business plans. Here is a sample business plan for Jolly's Java, a start-up bakery and coffee shop, courtesy of BPlans.

Jolly's Java—Sample Plan

This sample business plan was created using Business Plan Pro®, business planning software published by Palo Alto Software.

This plan may be edited using Business Plan Pro and is one of 500+ sample plans available from within the software.

To learn more about Business Plan Pro and other planning products for small- and medium-sized businesses, visit us at www.paloalto.com.

This is a sample business plan and the names, locations and numbers may have been changed, and substantial portions of the original plan text may have been omitted to preserve confidentiality and proprietary information.

You are welcome to use this plan as a starting point to create your own, but you do not have permission to resell, reproduce, publish, distribute or even copy this plan as it exists here.

Requests for reprints, academic use and other dissemination of this sample plan should be e-mailed to the marketing department of Palo Alto Software at marketing@paloalto.com. For product information visit our website: www.paloalto.com or call: 1-800-229-7526.

Confidentiality Agreement

The undersigned reader acknowledges that the information provided by
_____ in this business plan is confidential; there-
fore, reader agrees not to disclose it without the express written permission
of _____.

It is acknowledged by reader that information to be furnished in this business plan is in all respects confidential in nature, other than information
which is in the public domain through other means and that any disclosure
or use of same by reader, may cause serious harm or damage to

_____.

Upon request, this document is to be immediately returned to

_____.

_____

Signature

_____

Name (typed or printed)

_____

Date

This is a business plan. It does not imply an offering of securities.

Table of Contents

1.0 Executive Summary

Introduction

Jolly's Java and Bakery (JJB) is a start-up coffee and bakery retail establishment located in southwest Washington. JJB expects to catch the interest of a regular loyal customer base with its broad variety of coffee and pastry products. The company plans to build a strong market position in the town, due to the partners' industry experience and the mild competitive climate in the area.

JJB aims to offer its products at a competitive price to meet the demand of the middle- to higher-income local market area residents and tourists.

The Company

JJB is incorporated in the state of Washington. It is equally owned and managed by its two partners.

Austin Patterson has extensive experience in sales, marketing, and management, and was vice president of marketing with both Jansonne & Jansonne and Burper Foods. David Fields brings experience in the area of finance and administration, including a stint as chief financial officer with both Flaxfield Roasters and the national coffee store chain BuzzCups.

The company intends to hire two full-time pastry bakers and six part-time baristas to handle customer service and day-to-day operations.

Products and Services

JJB offers a broad range of coffee and espresso products, all from high-quality Columbian-grown imported coffee beans. JJB caters to all of its customers by providing each customer coffee and espresso products made to suit the customer, down to the smallest detail.

The bakery provides freshly prepared bakery and pastry products at all times during business operations. Six to eight moderate batches of bakery and pastry products are prepared during the day to ensure that fresh baked goods are always available.

Financial Considerations

JJB expects to raise $110,000 of its own capital, and to borrow $100,000 guaranteed by the SBA as a ten-year loan. This provides the bulk of the current financing required.

JJB anticipates sales of about $491,000 in the first year, $567,000 in the second year, and $655,000 in the third year of the plan. JJB should break even by the fourth month of its operation as it steadily increases its sales. Profits for this time period are expected to be approximately $12,000 in year 1, $36,000 by year 2, and $46,000 by year 3. The company does not anticipate any cash flow problems.

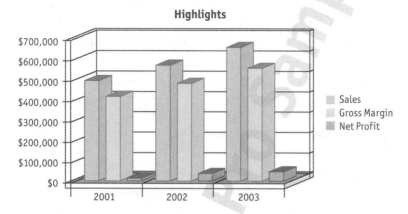

Highlights

1.1 **Mission**

JJB aims to offer high-quality coffee, espresso, and pastry products at a competitive price to meet the demand of the middle- to higher-income local market area residents and tourists.

1.2 **Keys to Success**

Keys to success for JJB will include:

1. Providing the highest-quality product with personal customer service.

2. Competitive pricing.

2.0 **Company Summary**

JJB is a bakery and coffee shop managed by two partners. These partners represent sales/management and finance/administration areas, respectively. The partners will provide funding from their own savings, which will cover start-up expenses and provide a financial cushion for the first months of operation. A ten-year Small Business Administration (SBA) loan will cover the rest of the required financing. The company plans to build a strong market position in the town, due to the partners' industry experience and mild competitive climate in the area.

2.1 Company Ownership

JJB is incorporated in the state of Washington. It is equally owned by its two partners.

2.2 Company History

JJB is a start-up company. Financing will come from the partners' capital and a ten-year SBA loan. The following chart and table illustrate the company's projected initial start-up costs.

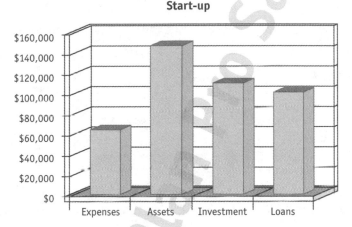

Start-up

3.0 Product/Service Description

JJB offers a broad range of coffee and espresso products, all from high-quality Columbian-grown imported coffee beans. JJB caters to all of its customers by providing each customer coffee and espresso products made to suit the customer, down to the smallest detail.

The bakery provides freshly prepared bakery and pastry products at all times during business operations. Six to eight moderate batches of bakery and pastry products are prepared during the day to ensure fresh baked goods are always available.

4.0 Market Analysis

JJB's focus is on meeting the demand of a regular local resident customer base as well as a significant level of tourist traffic from nearby highways.

4.1 Market Segmentation

JJB focuses on the middle- and upper-income markets. These market segments consume the majority of coffee and espresso products.

Local Residents

JJB wants to establish a large regular customer base. This will establish a healthy, consistent revenue base to ensure stability of the business.

Tourists

Tourist traffic composes approximately 35 percent of the revenues. High visibility and competitive products and service are critical to capture this segment of the market.

4.1.1 Market Analysis

The chart and table below outline the total market potential of the above described customer segments.

4.2 Target Market Segment Strategy

The dominant target market for JJB is a regular stream of local residents. Personal and expedient customer service at a competitive price is key to maintaining the local market share of this target market.

4.2.1 Market Needs

Because Washington has a cool climate for eight months out of the year, hot coffee products are very much in demand. During the remaining warmer four months of the year, iced coffee products are in significantly high demand, along with a slower but consistent demand for hot coffee products. Much of the day's activity occurs in the morning hours before ten a.m., with a relatively steady flow for the remainder of the day.

4.3 Service Business Analysis

The retail coffee industry in the U.S. has recently experienced rapid growth. The cool marine climate in southwest Washington stimulates consumption of hot beverages throughout the year. Coffee drinkers in the Pacific Northwest are finicky about the quality of beverages offered at the numerous coffee bars across the region. Despite low competition in the immediate area, JJB will position itself as a place where customers can enjoy a cup of delicious coffee with a fresh pastry in a relaxing environment.

4.3.1 Competition and Buying Patterns

Competition in the local area is somewhat sparse and does not provide nearly the level of product quality and customer service as JJB. Local customers are looking for a high-quality product in a relaxing atmosphere. They desire a unique, classy experience.

Leading competitors purchase and roast high-quality, whole-bean coffees and, along with Italian-style espresso beverages, cold-blended beverages, a variety of pastries and confections, coffee-related accessories and equipment, and a line of premium teas, and sell these items primarily through company-operated retail stores. In addition to sales through company-operated retail stores, leading competitors sell coffee and tea products through other channels of distribution (specialty operations).

Larger chains vary their product mix depending upon the size of each store and its location. Larger stores carry a broad selection of whole-bean coffees in various sizes and types of packaging as well as an assortment of coffee- and espresso-making equipment and accessories such as coffee grinders, coffeemakers, espresso machines, coffee filters, storage containers, travel tumblers and mugs. Smaller stores and kiosks typically sell a full line of coffee beverages, a more limited selection of whole-bean coffees, and a few accessories such as travel tumblers and logo mugs. During fiscal year 2000, industry retail sales mix by product type was approximately 73 percent beverages, 14 percent food items, 8 percent whole-bean coffees, and 5 percent coffee-making equipment and accessories.

Technologically savvy competitors make fresh coffee and coffee-related products conveniently available via mail order and online. Additionally, mail-order catalogs offering coffees, certain food items, and select coffee-making equipment and accessories have been made available by a few larger competitors. Websites offering online stores that allow customers to browse for and purchase coffee, gifts, and other items via the Internet have become more commonplace as well.

5.0 Strategy and Implementation

JJB will succeed by offering consumers high quality coffee, espresso, and bakery products with personal service at a competitive price.

5.1 Competitive Edge

JJB's competitive edge is the relatively low level of competition in the local area in this particular niche.

5.2 Marketing Strategy

As the chart and table show, JJB anticipates sales of about $491,000 in the first year, $567,105 in the second year, and $655,006 in the third year of the plan.

Table: Sales Forecast

Sales Forecast

Unit Sales	2001	2002	2003
Espresso Drinks	135,000	148,500	163,350
Pastry Items	86,000	94,600	104,060
Other	0	0	0
Total Unit Sales	221,000	243,100	267,410

Unit Prices	2001	2002	2003
Espresso Drinks	$3.00	$3.15	$3.31
Pastry Items	$1.00	$1.05	$1.10
Other	$0.00	$0.00	$0.00

Sales			
Espresso Drinks	$405,000	$467,775	$540,280
Pastry Items	$86,000	$99,330	$114,726
Other	$0	$0	$0
Total Sales	$491,000	$567,105	$655,006

Direct Unit Costs	2001	2002	2003
Espresso Drinks	$0.25	$0.26	$0.28
Pastry Items	$0.50	$0.53	$0.55
Other	$0.00	$0.00	$0.00

Direct Cost of Sales	2001	2002	2003
Espresso Drinks	$33,750	$38,981	$45,023
Pastry Items	$43,000	$49,665	$57,363
Other	$0	$0	$0
Subtotal Direct Cost of Sales	$76,750	$88,646	$102,386

Sales Monthly

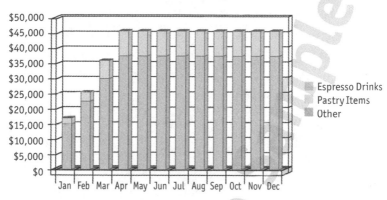

Sales by Year

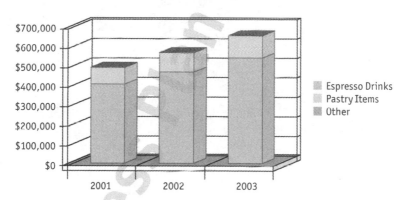

6.0 Management Team

Austin Patterson has extensive experience in sales, marketing, and management, and was vice president of marketing with both Jansonne & Jansonne and Burper Foods. David Fields brings experience in the area of finance and administration, including a stint as chief financial officer with both Flaxfield Roasters and the national coffee store chain BuzzCups.

6.1 Personnel Plan

As the personnel plan shows, JJB expects to make significant investments in sales, sales support, and product development personnel.

Table: Personnel

Personnel Plan

	2001	2002	2003
Managers	$100,000	$105,000	$110,250
Pastry Bakers	$40,800	$42,840	$44,982
Baristas	$120,000	$126,000	$132,300
Other	$0	$0	$0
Total People	10	10	10
Total Payroll	$260,800	$273,840	$287,532

7.0 Financial Plan

JJB expects to raise $110,000 of its own capital, and to borrow $100,000 guaranteed by the SBA as a ten-year loan. This provides the bulk of the current financing required.

7.1 Break-even Analysis

JJB's Break-even Analysis is based on the average of the first-year figures for total sales units, and by operating expenses. These are presented as per-unit revenue, per-unit costs, and fixed costs. These conservative assumptions make for a more accurate estimate of real risk. JJB should break even by the fourth month of its operation as it steadily increases its sales.

Break-even Analysis

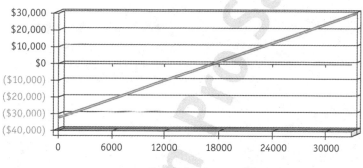

Monthly break-even point

Break-even point = where line intersects with 0

Table: Break-even Analysis

Break-even Analysis:

Monthly Units Break-even	17,483
Monthly Revenue Break-even	$38,462

Assumptions:

Average Per-Unit Revenue	$2.20
Average Per-Unit Variable Cost	$0.35
Estimated Monthly Fixed Cost	$32,343

7.2 Projected Profit and Loss

As the Profit and Loss table shows, JJB expects to continue its steady growth in profitability over the next three years of operations.

Table: Profit and Loss

Pro Forma Profit and Loss

	2001	2002	2003
Sales	$491,000	$567,105	$655,006
Direct Costs of Goods	$76,750	$88,646	$102,386
Other	$0	$0	$0
Cost of Goods Sold	$76,750	$88,646	$102,386
Gross Margin	$414,250	$478,459	$552,620
Gross Margin %	84.37%	84.37%	84.37%
Expenses:			
Payroll	$260,800	$273,840	$287,532
Sales and Marketing and Other Expenses	$27,000	$35,200	$71,460
Depreciation	$60,000	$69,000	$79,350
Utilities	$1,200	$1,260	$1,323
Payroll Taxes	$39,120	$41,076	$43,130
Other	$0	$0	$0
Total Operating Expenses	$388,120	$420,376	$482,795
Profit Before Interest and Taxes	$26,130	$58,083	$69,825
Interest Expense	$10,000	$9,500	$8,250
Taxes Incurred	$4,033	$12,146	$15,394
Net Profit	$12,098	$36,437	$46,181
Net Profit/Sales	2.46%	6.43%	7.05%
Include Negative Taxes	TRUE	TRUE	TRUE

7.3 Projected Cash Flow

The cash flow projection shows that provisions for ongoing expenses are ad-
equate to meet JJB's needs as the business generates cash flow sufficient to
support operations.

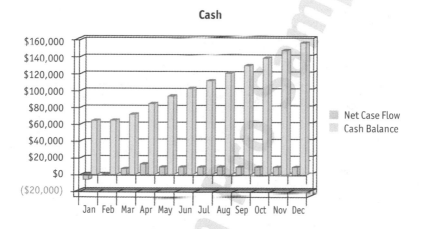

Cash

Table: Cash Flow

Pro Forma Cash Flow	2001	2002	2003
Cash Received			
Cash from Operations:			
Cash Sales	$491,000	$567,105	$655,006
Cash from Receivables	$0	$0	$0
Subtotal Cash from Operations	$491,000	$567,105	$655,006
Additional Cash Received			
Non Operating (Other) Income	$0	$0	$0
Sales Tax, VAT, HST/GST Received	$0	$0	$0
New Current Borrowing	$0	$0	$0
New Other Liabilities (interest-free)	$0	$0	$0
New Long-term Liabilities	$0	$0	$0
Sales of Other Current Assets	$0	$0	$0
Sales of Long-term Assets	$0	$0	$0
New Investment Received	$0	$0	$0
Subtotal Cash Received	$491,000	$567,105	$655,006
Expenditures	2001	2002	2003
Expenditures from Operations:			
Cash Spending	$13,071	$17,907	$23,175
Payment of Accounts Payable	$395,701	$439,643	$501,815
Subtotal Spent on Operations	$408,772	$457,550	$524,989
Additional Cash Spent			
Non Operating (Other) Expense	$0	$0	$0
Sales Tax, VAT, HST/GST Paid Out	$0	$0	$0
Principal Repayment of Current Borrowing	$0	$0	$0
Other Liabilities Principal Repayment	$0	$0	$0
Long-term Liabilities Principal Repayment	$0	$10,000	$15,000
Purchase Other Current Assets	$0	$0	$0
Purchase Long-term Assets	$0	$20,000	$20,000
Dividends	$0	$0	$0
Subtotal Cash Spent	$408,772	$487,550	$559,989
Net Cash Flow	$82,228	$79,555	$95,017
Cash Balance	$152,228	$231,783	$326,800

7.4 Balance Sheet

The following is a projected Balance Sheet for JJB.

Table: Balance Sheet

Pro Forma Balance Sheet

Assets

Current Assets	2001	2002	2003
Cash	$152,228	$231,783	$326,800
Other Current Assets	$12,000	$12,000	$12,000
Total Current Assets	$164,228	$243,783	$338,800
Long-term Assets			
Long-term Assets	$65,000	$85,000	$105,000
Accumulated Depreciation	$60,000	$129,000	$208,350
Total Long-term Assets	$5,000	($44,000)	($103,350)
Total Assets	$169,228	$199,783	$235,450

Liabilities and Capital

	2001	2002	2003
Accounts Payable	$11,131	$15,248	$19,734
Current Borrowing	$0	$0	$0
Other Current Liabilities	$0	$0	$0
Subtotal Current Liabilities	$11,131	$15,248	$19,734
Long-term Liabilities	$100,000	$90,000	$75,000
Total Liabilities	$111,131	$105,248	$94,734
Paid-in Capital	$110,000	$110,000	$110,000
Retained Earnings	($64,000)	($51,903)	($15,465)
Earnings	$12,098	$36,437	$46,181
Total Capital	$58,098	$94,535	$140,716
Total Liabilities and Capital	$169,228	$199,783	$235,450
Net Worth	$58,098	$94,535	$140,716

7.5 Business Ratios

The following table represents key ratios for the retail bakery and coffee shop industry. The ratios are determined by the Standard Industry Classification (SIC) Index code 5812, Eating Places.

Table: Ratios

Ratio Analysis

	2001	2002	2003	Industry Profile
Sales Growth	0.00%	15.50%	15.50%	7.60%
Percent of Total Assets				
Accounts Receivable	0.00%	0.00%	0.00%	4.50%
Inventory	0.00%	0.00%	0.00%	3.60%
Other Current Assets	7.09%	6.01%	5.10%	35.60%
Total Current Assets	97.05%	122.02%	143.89%	43.70%
Long-term Assets	2.95%	−22.02%	−43.89%	56.30%
Total Assets	100.00%	100.00%	100.00%	100.00%
Current Liabilities	0.00%	0.00%	0.00%	32.70%
Long-term Liabilities	59.09%	45.05%	31.85%	28.50%
Total Liabilities	59.09%	45.05%	31.85%	61.20%
Net Worth	40.91%	54.95%	68.15%	38.80%
Percent of Sales				
Sales	100.00%	100.00%	100.00%	100.00%
Gross Margin	84.37%	84.37%	84.37%	60.50%
Selling, General & Administrative Expenses	74.74%	71.43%	71.39%	39.80%
Advertising Expenses	0.49%	1.76%	6.87%	3.20%
Profit Before Interest and Taxes	5.32%	10.24%	10.66%	0.70%
Main Ratios				
Current	14.75	15.99	17.17	0.98
Quick	14.75	15.99	17.17	0.65
Total Debt to Total Assets	65.67%	52.68%	40.24%	61.20%
Pre-tax Return on Net Worth	27.76%	51.39%	43.76%	1.70%
Pre-tax Return on Assets	9.53%	24.32%	26.15%	4.30%

(continues on next page)

Table: Ratios *(continued)*

Business Vitality Profile	2001	2002	2003	Industry
Sales per Employee	$49,100	$56,711	$65,501	$0
Survival Rate				0.00%
Additional Ratios				
Net Profit Margin	2.46%	6.43%	7.05%	n.a
Return on Equity	20.82%	38.54%	32.82%	n.a
Activity Ratios				
Accounts Receivable				
Turnover	0.00	0.00	0.00	n.a
Collection Days	0	0	0	n.a
Inventory Turnover	0.00	0.00	0.00	n.a
Accounts Payable				
Turnover	36.46	29.10	25.66	n.a
Payment Days	8	130	151	
Total Asset Turnover	2.90	2.84	2.78	n.a
Debt Ratios				
Debt to Net Worth	1.91	1.11	0.67	n.a
Current Liab. to Liab.	0.10	0.14	0.21	n.a
Liquidity Ratios				
Net Working Capital	$153,098	$228,535	$319,066	n.a
Interest Coverage	2.61	6.11	8.46	n.a
Additional Ratios				
Assets to Sales	0.34	0.35	0.36	n.a
Current Debt/Total Assets	7%	8%	8%	n.a
Acid Test	14.75	15.99	17.17	n.a
Sales/Net Worth	8.45	6.00	4.65	n.a
Dividend Payout	0.00	0.00	0.00	n.a

Appendix Table: Sales Forecast

Sales Forecast

Unit Sales	Jan	Feb	Mar	Apr	May
Espresso Drinks	5,000	7,500	10,000	12,500	12,500
Pastry Items	2,000	3,000	6,000	8,333	8,333
Other	0	0	0	0	0
Total Unit Sales	7,000	10,500	16,000	20,833	20,833

Unit Prices	Jan	Feb	Mar	Apr	May
Espresso Drinks	$3.00	$3.00	$3.00	$3.00	$3.00
Pastry Items	$1.00	$1.00	$1.00	$1.00	$1.00
Other	$0.00	$0.00	$0.00	$0.00	$0.00

Sales					
Espresso Drinks	$15,000	$22,500	$30,000	$37,500	$37,500
Pastry Items	$2,000	$3,000	$6,000	$8,333	$8,333
Other	$0	$0	$0	$0	$0
Total Sales	$17,000	$25,500	$36,000	$45,833	$45,833

Direct Unit Costs	Jan	Feb	Mar	Apr	May
Espresso Drinks	$0.25	$0.25	$0.25	$0.25	$0.25
Pastry Items	$0.50	$0.50	$0.50	$0.50	$0.50
Other	$0.00	$0.00	$0.00	$0.00	$0.00

Direct Cost of Sales	Jan	Feb	Mar	Apr	May
Espresso Drinks	$1,250	$1,875	$2,500	$3,125	$3,125
Pastry Items	$1,000	$1,500	$3,000	$4,167	$4,167
Other	$0	$0	$0	$0	$0
Subtotal Direct Cost of Sales	$2,250	$3,375	$5,500	$7,292	$7,292

	Jun	Jul	Aug	Sep	Oct	Nov	Dec
	12,500	12,500	12,500	12,500	12,500	12,500	12,500
	8,333	8,333	8,333	8,333	8,333	8,333	8,333
	0	0	0	0	0	0	0
	20,833	20,833	20,833	20,833	20,833	20,833	20,833

	Jun	Jul	Aug	Sep	Oct	Nov	Dec
	$3.00	$3.00	$3.00	$3.00	$3.00	$3.00	$3.00
	$1.00	$1.00	$1.00	$1.00	$1.00	$1.00	$1.00
	$0.00	$0.00	$0.00	$0.00	$0.00	$0.00	$0.00

	Jun	Jul	Aug	Sep	Oct	Nov	Dec
	$37,500	$37,500	$37,500	$37,500	$37,500	$37,500	$37,500
	$8,333	$8,333	$8,333	$8,333	$8,333	$8,333	$8,333
	$0	$0	$0	$0	$0	$0	$0
	$45,833	$45,833	$45,833	$45,833	$45,833	$45,833	$45,833

	Jun	Jul	Aug	Sep	Oct	Nov	Dec
	$0.25	$0.25	$0.25	$0.25	$0.25	$0.25	$0.25
	$0.50	$0.50	$0.50	$0.50	$0.50	$0.50	$0.50
	$0.00	$0.00	$0.00	$0.00	$0.00	$0.00	$0.00

	Jun	Jul	Aug	Sep	Oct	Nov	Dec
	$3,125	$3,125	$3,125	$3,125	$3,125	$3,125	$3,125
	$4,167	$4,167	$4,167	$4,167	$4,167	$4,167	$4,167
	$0	$0	$0	$0	$0	$0	$0
	$7,292	$7,292	$7,292	$7,292	$7,292	$7,292	$7,292

Appendix Table: Personnel

Personnel Plan

	Jan	Feb	Mar	Apr	May
Managers	$8,333	$8,333	$8,333	$8,333	$8,333
Pastry Bakers	$3,400	$3,400	$3,400	$3,400	$3,400
Baristas	$10,000	$10,000	$10,000	$10,000	$10,000
Other	$0	$0	$0	$0	$0
Total People	10	10	10	10	10
Total Payroll	$21,733	$21,733	$21,733	$21,733	$21,733

Jun	Jul	Aug	Sep	Oct	Nov	Dec
$8,333	$8,333	$8,333	$8,333	$8,333	$8,333	$8,333
$3,400	$3,400	$3,400	$3,400	$3,400	$3,400	$3,400
$10,000	$10,000	$10,000	$10,000	$10,000	$10,000	$10,000
$0	$0	$0	$0	$0	$0	$0
10	10	10	10	10	10	10
$21,733	$21,733	$21,733	$21,733	$21,733	$21,733	$21,733

Appendix Table: General Assumptions

General Assumptions

	Jan	Feb	Mar	Apr	May
Plan Month	1	2	3	4	5
Current Interest Rate	10.00%	10.00%	10.00%	10.00%	10.00%
Long-term Interest Rate	10.00%	10.00%	10.00%	10.00%	10.00%
Tax Rate	25.00%	25.00%	25.00%	25.00%	25.00%
Other	0.00%	0.00%	0.00%	0.00%	0.00%
Calculated Totals					
Payroll Expense	$21,733	$21,733	$21,733	$21,733	$21,733
New Accounts Payable	$25,640	$28,311	$32,108	$35,530	$35,530

	Jun	Jul	Aug	Sep	Oct	Nov	Dec
	6	7	8	9	10	11	12
	10.00%	10.00%	10.00%	10.00%	10.00%	10.00%	10.00%
	10.00%	10.00%	10.00%	10.00%	10.00%	10.00%	10.00%
	25.00%	25.00%	25.00%	25.00%	25.00%	25.00%	25.00%
	0.00%	0.00%	0.00%	0.00%	0.00%	0.00%	0.00%
	$21,733	$21,733	$21,733	$21,733	$21,733	$21,733	$21,733
	$35,530	$35,530	$35,530	$35,530	$35,530	$35,530	$35,530

Appendix Table: Profit and Loss

Pro Forma Profit and Loss

		Jan	Feb	Mar	Apr	May
Sales		$17,000	$25,500	$36,000	$45,833	$45,833
Direct Costs of Goods		$2,250	$3,375	$5,500	$7,292	$7,292
Other		$0	$0	$0	$0	$0
Cost of Goods Sold		$2,250	$3,375	$5,500	$7,292	$7,292
Gross Margin		$14,750	$22,125	$30,500	$38,542	$38,542
Gross Margin %		86.76%	86.76%	84.72%	84.09%	84.09%
Expenses:						
Payroll		$21,733	$21,733	$21,733	$21,733	$21,733
Sales and Marketing and Other Expenses		$2,250	$2,250	$2,250	$2,250	$2,250
Depreciation	15%	$5,000	$5,000	$5,000	$5,000	$5,000
Utilities	5%	$100	$100	$100	$100	$100
Payroll Taxes	15%	$3,260	$3,260	$3,260	$3,260	$3,260
Other		$0	$0	$0	$0	$0
Total Operating Expenses		$32,343	$32,343	$32,343	$32,343	$32,343
Profit Before Interest and Taxes		($17,593)	($10,218)	($1,843)	$6,198	$6,198
Interest Expense		$833	$833	$833	$833	$833
Taxes Incurred		($4,607)	($2,763)	($669)	$1,341	$1,341
Net Profit		($13,820)	($8,289)	($2,008)	$4,024	$4,024
Net Profit/Sales		−81.29%	−32.50%	−5.58%	8.78%	8.78%
Include Negative Taxes						

Jun	Jul	Aug	Sep	Oct	Nov	Dec
$45,833	$45,833	$45,833	$45,833	$45,833	$45,833	$45,833
$7,292	$7,292	$7,292	$7,292	$7,292	$7,292	$7,292
$0	$0	$0	$0	$0	$0	$0
$7,292	$7,292	$7,292	$7,292	$7,292	$7,292	$7,292
$38,542	$38,542	$38,542	$38,542	$38,542	$38,542	$38,542
84.09%	84.09%	84.09%	84.09%	84.09%	84.09%	84.09%
$21,733	$21,733	$21,733	$21,733	$21,733	$21,733	$21,733
$2,250	$2,250	$2,250	$2,250	$2,250	$2,250	$2,250
$5,000	$5,000	$5,000	$5,000	$5,000	$5,000	$5,000
$100	$100	$100	$100	$100	$100	$100
$3,260	$3,260	$3,260	$3,260	$3,260	$3,260	$3,260
$0	$0	$0	$0	$0	$0	$0
$32,343	$32,343	$32,343	$32,343	$32,343	$32,343	$32,343
$6,198	$6,198	$6,198	$6,198	$6,198	$6,198	$6,198
$833	$833	$833	$833	$833	$833	$833
$1,341	$1,341	$1,341	$1,341	$1,341	$1,341	$1,341
$4,024	$4,024	$4,024	$4,024	$4,024	$4,024	$4,024
8.78%	8.78%	8.78%	8.78%	8.78%	8.78%	8.78%

Appendix Table: Cash Flow

Pro Forma Cash Flow

		Jan	Feb	Mar	Apr
Cash Received					
Cash from Operations:					
Cash Sales		$17,000	$25,500	$36,000	$45,833
Cash from Receivables		$0	$0	$0	$0
Subtotal Cash from Operations		$17,000	$25,500	$36,000	$45,833
Additional Cash Received					
Non Operating (Other) Income		$0	$0	$0	$0
Sales Tax, VAT, HST/GST Received	0.00%	$0	$0	$0	$0
New Current Borrowing		$0	$0	$0	$0
New Other Liabilities (interest-free)		$0	$0	$0	$0
New Long-term Liabilities		$0	$0	$0	$0
Sales of Other Current Assets		$0	$0	$0	$0
Sales of Long-term Assets		$0	$0	$0	$0
New Investment Received		$0	$0	$0	$0
Subtotal Cash Received		$17,000	$25,500	$36,000	$45,833
Expenditures		Jan	Feb	Mar	Apr
Expenditures from Operations:					
Cash Spending		$180	$477	$899	$1,279
Payment of Accounts Payable		$25,070	$25,729	$28,438	$32,222
Subtotal Spent on Operations		$25,250	$26,206	$29,337	$33,502
Additional Cash Spent					
Non Operating (Other) Expense		$0	$0	$0	$0
Sales Tax, VAT, HST/GST Paid Out		$0	$0	$0	$0
Principal Repayment of Current Borrowing		$0	$0	$0	$0
Other Liabilities Principal Repayment		$0	$0	$0	$0
Long-term Liabilities Principal Repayment		$0	$0	$0	$0
Purchase Other Current Assets		$0	$0	$0	$0
Purchase Long-term Assets		$0	$0	$0	$0
Dividends		$0	$0	$0	$0
Subtotal Cash Spent		$25,250	$26,206	$29,337	$33,502
Net Cash Flow		($8,250)	($706)	$6,663	$12,332
Cash Balance		$61,750	$61,044	$67,707	$80,038

May	Jun	Jul	Aug	Sep	Oct	Nov	Dec
$45,833	$45,833	$45,833	$45,833	$45,833	$45,833	$45,833	$45,833
$0	$0	$0	$0	$0	$0	$0	$0
$45,833	$45,833	$45,833	$45,833	$45,833	$45,833	$45,833	$45,833
$0	$0	$0	$0	$0	$0	$0	$0
$0	$0	$0	$0	$0	$0	$0	$0
$0	$0	$0	$0	$0	$0	$0	$0
$0	$0	$0	$0	$0	$0	$0	$0
$0	$0	$0	$0	$0	$0	$0	$0
$0	$0	$0	$0	$0	$0	$0	$0
$0	$0	$0	$0	$0	$0	$0	$0
$0	$0	$0	$0	$0	$0	$0	$0
$45,833	$45,833	$45,833	$45,833	$45,833	$45,833	$45,833	$45,833
May	Jun	Jul	Aug	Sep	Oct	Nov	Dec

May	Jun	Jul	Aug	Sep	Oct	Nov	Dec
$1,279	$1,279	$1,279	$1,279	$1,279	$1,279	$1,279	$1,279
$35,530	$35,530	$35,530	$35,530	$35,530	$35,530	$35,530	$35,530
$36,810	$36,810	$36,810	$36,810	$36,810	$36,810	$36,810	$36,810
$0	$0	$0	$0	$0	$0	$0	$0
$0	$0	$0	$0	$0	$0	$0	$0
$0	$0	$0	$0	$0	$0	$0	$0
$0	$0	$0	$0	$0	$0	$0	$0
$0	$0	$0	$0	$0	$0	$0	$0
$0	$0	$0	$0	$0	$0	$0	$0
$0	$0	$0	$0	$0	$0	$0	$0
$0	$0	$0	$0	$0	$0	$0	$0
$36,810	$36,810	$36,810	$36,810	$36,810	$36,810	$36,810	$36,810
$9,024	$9,024	$9,024	$9,024	$9,024	$9,024	$9,024	$9,024
$89,062	$98,086	$107,109	$116,133	$125,157	$134,181	$143,204	$152,228

Appendix Table: Balance Sheet

Pro Forma Balance Sheet

Assets

Current Assets	Starting Balances	Jan	Feb	Mar	Apr	May
Cash	$70,000	$61,750	$61,044	$67,707	$80,038	$89,062
Other Current Assets	$12,000	$12,000	$12,000	$12,000	$12,000	$12,000
Total Current Assets	$82,000	$73,750	$73,044	$79,707	$92,038	$101,062
Long-term Assets						
Long-term Assets	$65,000	$65,000	$65,000	$65,000	$65,000	$65,000
Accumulated Depreciation	$0	$5,000	$10,000	$15,000	$20,000	$25,000
Total Long-term Assets	$65,000	$60,000	$55,000	$50,000	$45,000	$40,000
Total Assets	$147,000	$133,750	$128,044	$129,707	$137,038	$141,062

Liabilities and Capital		Jan	Feb	Mar	Apr	May
Accounts Payable	$1,000	$1,570	$4,152	$7,823	$11,131	$11,131
Current Borrowing	$0	$0	$0	$0	$0	$0
Other Current Liabilities	$0	$0	$0	$0	$0	$0
Subtotal Current Liabilities	$1,000	$1,570	$4,152	$7,823	$11,131	$11,131
Long-term Liabilities	$100,000	$100,000	$100,000	$100,000	$100,000	$100,000
Total Liabilities	$101,000	$101,570	$104,152	$107,823	$111,131	$111,131
Paid-in Capital	$110,000	$110,000	$110,000	$110,000	$110,000	$110,000
Retained Earnings	($64,000)	($64,000)	($64,000)	($64,000)	($64,000)	($64,000)
Earnings	$0	($13,820)	($22,109)	($24,116)	($20,093)	($16,069)
Total Capital	$46,000	$32,180	$23,891	$21,884	$25,908	$29,931
Total Liabilities and Capital	$147,000	$133,750	$128,044	$129,707	$137,038	$141,062
Net Worth	$46,000	$32,180	$23,891	$21,884	$25,908	$29,931

	Jun	Jul	Aug	Sep	Oct	Nov	Dec
	$98,086	$107,109	$116,133	$125,157	$134,181	$143,204	$152,228
	$12,000	$12,000	$12,000	$12,000	$12,000	$12,000	$12,000
	$110,086	$119,109	$128,133	$137,157	$146,181	$155,204	$164,228
	$65,000	$65,000	$65,000	$65,000	$65,000	$65,000	$65,000
	$30,000	$35,000	$40,000	$45,000	$50,000	$55,000	$60,000
	$35,000	$30,000	$25,000	$20,000	$15,000	$10,000	$5,000
	$145,086	$149,109	$153,133	$157,157	$161,181	$165,204	$169,228

	Jun	Jul	Aug	Sep	Oct	Nov	Dec
	$11,131	$11,131	$11,131	$11,131	$11,131	$11,131	$11,131
	$0	$0	$0	$0	$0	$0	$0
	$0	$0	$0	$0	$0	$0	$0
	$11,131	$11,131	$11,131	$11,131	$11,131	$11,131	$11,131
	$100,000	$100,000	$100,000	$100,000	$100,000	$100,000	$100,000
	$111,131	$111,131	$111,131	$111,131	$111,131	$111,131	$111,131
	$110,000	$110,000	$110,000	$110,000	$110,000	$110,000	$110,000
	($64,000)	($64,000)	($64,000)	($64,000)	($64,000)	($64,000)	($64,000)
	($12,045)	($8,021)	($3,997)	$26	$4,050	$8,074	$12,098
	$33,955	$37,979	$42,003	$46,026	$50,050	$54,074	$58,098
	$145,086	$149,109	$153,133	$157,157	$161,181	$165,204	$169,228
	$33,955	$37,979	$42,003	$46,026	$50,050	$54,074	$58,098

BETTER BUSINESS BUREAU WORKSHEETS FOR ESTIMATING START-UP COSTS

Entrepreneurs often underestimate the amount of capital they'll need to start and run a business, so getting your costs down on paper is critical. A number of resources can help you estimate start-up costs. SCORE, an affiliate of the Small Business Administration, provides tips on its website, while BPlans.com offers a starting-costs calculator. The following is a sample worksheet from the Better Business Bureau for estimating your intial outlay.

• • •

Estimating how much you will need to start your business requires a careful analysis of several factors. Put together a list of the various one-time initial costs of opening your doors—those expenses that you only have to pay once. Record them in the table on page 242.

TABLE 1	
	Amount of Cash Needed
START-UP EXPENSES	
Housing your business: First consider where you plan to house your business. Will you be constructing a building? Write down the amount of money per contractor bid and other one-time fees that will be associated with constructing the building. If you are purchasing a place of business, write down the purchase price if paid in full with cash. If you are going to rent office space, record the rental deposit (usually equal to one month's rent) that will need to be paid before opening.	$
Outfitting your place of business: Now take a look at what it will cost to outfit your business. You will need to consider the interior of your place of business as well as the exterior.	$
Fixtures: Write down the retail prices of any fixtures you will need to open your business. These might include counters, built-in storage shelves and cabinets and window display fixtures.	$
Transportation and installation of fixtures: Record the expenses you will incur to transport and install the fixtures identified above.	$
Office equipment: Now consider what office equipment you will need to operate your business. Under this category you will estimate the one-time cost, if paid in full with cash, of office computer hardware and software, printers, fax machines, copier machines, telephone and telephone systems, cash registers, office safe and delivery equipment, if needed. Record the cash down payment if you will be purchasing the equipment on contract.	$
Machinery equipment: If your business will require machinery or equipment to produce your product, record the one-time cost of purchasing that equipment, if paid in full with cash, or the cash down payment, if purchased on contract. If you will be leasing your equipment, record the lease fees that must be paid before opening.	$
Transportation and installation of equipment: Record what you expect to pay for the transportation and installation of your various pieces of equipment. Will you need to hire a computer consultant to advise you on	

	Amount of Cash Needed
START-UP EXPENSES	
your hardware needs, or to install software? What will contractors charge you to install cash registers, your business safe or other pieces of equipment?	$
Furniture: If you need office furnishings (desks, credenzas, file cabinets, bookcases, sofas, chairs, end tables, lamps), record the cost of each. If you're paying cash in full, enter the full retail price. If you are going to pay by installments, make note of the down payment as your start-up cost.	$
Decorating and remodeling: If your office space will need to be reconfigured, or you will need to redecorate, anticipate what you will spend to do so. Talk to suppliers with whom you plan to purchase these services, and record in this category the cash price of such services. If you are renting office space, sometimes you can negotiate with the landlord to include renovations in your base rent.	$
Business exterior: You may also incur some costs to prepare the exterior of your place of business for opening. Consider whether you will need to purchase outside signs or exterior lighting and record the cost. Anticipate other expenses you will incur to ensure an attractive, safe entry to your place of business.	$
YOUR PRODUCT	
Now it's time to consider the one-time costs related to the product or service your business will sell to customers.	$
Raw materials: If you are a manufacturer, you will need a supply of raw materials on hand so you can keep up with orders; record the dollar cost of the materials.	$
Beginning inventory: Record the dollar cost of the inventory you will need to open your business as well as the stock you will need to replenish until your business starts to bring in enough money to purchase inventory.	$
PROTECTING YOUR BUSINESS AND EMPLOYEES	
Insurance: Obtain a bid from your insurance agent for property insurance and other types of business insurance you will need. If you plan to offer your employees health insurance, talk to your agent about the up-front fee. Record the premium payment you will need to make before opening your business.	$

	Amount of Cash Needed
PROTECTING YOUR BUSINESS AND EMPLOYEES	
Office and employee security: If you will be engaging the services of an office security firm, record any up-front fees.	$
PROMOTING YOUR BUSINESS	
Advertising and promotion for your opening: Record the dollar cost of any initial advertising and marketing that you plan to do to announce the launch of your business. Include the cost of flyers, sales letters and calls, signs, brochures and other promotional items. Also, in this category include the cost for printing office letterhead and business cards.	$
OPERATING YOUR BUSINESS	
Deposits with public utilities: Record the cash you will need to establish telephone service, electricity and other public utilities. Include line connection charges, the cost of any inside and outside installation that might be required and any initial deposits.	$
Attorney, CPA and other professional fees: Determine what initial fees you will need to pay your attorney, accountant and any other professional to retain their services.	$
Business licenses and permits: Find out from local and city authorities the cost of any business license, building permit or name registration fees. If the product or service you sell is taxable, you will need to check with your state's department of taxation/revenue about the cost of a sales permit and any licenses the state may require.	$
Supplies: This category will include costs for purchasing office supplies (paper, pens, staplers, etc.), cleaning supplies and other supplies you and your employees will need in order to produce your product or provide services.	$
Services: Will you be hiring a cleaning service or a landscape service? If these services require a start-up fee or down payment, you'll want to record them with your start-up costs.	$
Unanticipated expenses: Include an estimate of cash that will be required for unexpected expenses or losses, special purchases and the like.	$

	Amount of Cash Needed
OPERATING YOUR BUSINESS	
Other: Miscellaneous expenses such as merchant association fees, amount of cash needed for the cash registers, bank service fees, etc., should be recorded here.	$
TOTAL START-UP COSTS FOR OPENING	$

Now you will want to consider the ongoing, recurring costs you will face each month. Write down the anticipated expense for one month in column 2 on page 246, based on sales of a specific amount per year. (As you review your financials each month, you'll be able to gauge whether you are on track to achieve your sales target. If not, then perhaps it will make sense to adjust your monthly expenses accordingly.) Multiply column 2 by six to obtain the six-month estimate of your operating expenses that experts recommend. This figure should be placed in column 3.

You'll want to consider both business *and* personal living expenses when determining how much cash you will need. If you are leaving a salaried job to start your business, you should include in your expense projection an estimate of your and your family's living costs for the months it will take to build your business. Talk to family members about the minimum amount of money your household will need each month to function. This figure should be inserted into the miscellaneous category in Table 2.

Ongoing expenses will typically include the following:

TABLE 2		
Estimated Monthly Expenses	Estimate of Monthly Expenses Based on Sales in $ Per Year	Multiply Amount in Column 2 by six
Column 1	Column 2	Column 3
EMPLOYEE EXPENSES		
Employee wages: In this category, include an estimate of your monthly salary as the owner-manager, as well as the salaries and wages of any other employees.	$	$
Payroll taxes, including Social Security	$	$
Health insurance (exclude any amount included in your Start-up Costs)	$	$
Workers' compensation insurance	$	$
HOUSING YOUR BUSINESS		
Monthly mortgage or rent payment	$	$
Building/landscape maintenance	$	$
PROTECTING YOUR BUSINESS		
Office and employee security (exclude any amount included in your Start-up Costs)	$	$
Business insurance (exclude any amount included in your Start-up Costs)	$	$
OUTFITTING YOUR BUSINESS		
Office supplies	$	$
Office equipment leases	$	$
Machinery lease payments	$	$
YOUR PRODUCT		
Inventory: Include amount required for inventory expansion.	$	$
Sales Tax	$	$

Estimated Monthly Expenses	Estimate of Monthly Expenses Based on Sales in $ Per Year	Multiply Amount in Column 2 by six
Column 1	Column 2	Column 3
PROMOTING YOUR BUSINESS		
Advertising and promotion: Monthly cost of yellow pages or other types of advertising, postage for mailing sales promotions, printing of leaflets, etc.	$	$
OPERATING YOUR BUSINESS		
Utilities: Telephone, DSL lines, electricity and other utilities. Include costs of cell phones and pagers.	$	$
Maintenance and repairs	$	$
Delivery/transportation expenses	$	$
Attorney, CPA and professional fees	$	$
Bank service fees	$	$
Loan payments: Principal and Interest	$	$
Credit card charges	$	$
Cleaning service (exclude any amount included in your Start-up Costs)	$	$
Miscellaneous: such as your family's living costs	$	$
TOTAL REPEATING COSTS	For One Month $	For Six Months $

TABLE 3		
Final Tally of Capital Requirement		
Total Start-up Costs	Insert Total Amount from Table 1	$
Six Months' Repeating Costs	Insert Total Amount from Table 2	$
TOTAL CASH NEEDED		$

Source: Better Business Bureau

ACKNOWLEDGMENTS

I always thought that if I wrote a book, I'd thank the English teachers who taught me how to read, write and string words together in a way that made sense to others. So many thanks to Ms. Jennifer Foster, Mrs. Janice Dowling, Ms. Marcia Hayden-Horan and Professor Natalia Rachel Singer.

I'm grateful for supportive bosses—Linda Fung at Dow Jones, Ray Hennessey and Stephanie AuWerter at *SmartMoney*, Kimberly Weisul at *BusinessWeek* and Kevin Delaney at *The Wall Street Journal*—for having such confidence in me. And a big shout-out to a fantastic Crown editor, Lindsay Orman, and *Wall Street Journal* books editor, Roe D'Angelo, and to Kaja Whitehouse who steered me in Roe's direction.

I've had the good fortune of spending time with loving people who showed me a thing or two about running a business, among other things. Many thanks to my mother, who was the CEO of our household and my father, who was a self-employed attorney. I learned firsthand about the trials and tribulations of running a business through another important person, Phil Polomsky, who started a sandwich shop in Chicago. And a special thank-you to Rodger Fairey, who was a steady companion throughout the writing of this book and—lucky for me—a self-employed architect who shared his thoughts and experience, usually over a great bottle of wine.

I need to give props to Pam Squillaro, who encouraged me to write about women and personal finance, which actually led me to write about business owners. My lasting appreciation goes to *SmartMoney*'s Aleks Todorova, who agreed to read some early chapters and supplied me with excellent feedback while—unbeknownst to me—she was in active labor with her son. And because I told him I would, thank you to D. G. for getting me through it all.

And of course, thank you to all the entrepreneurs who trusted me with their stories and who continue to inspire me with their fearlessness, ambition and, above all, enthusiasm.

INDEX

ABOUT THE AUTHOR

COLLEEN DEBAISE is small business editor at *The Wall Street Journal*. Prior to that, she was deputy editor at *BusinessWeek SmallBiz* and editor at SMSmallBiz.com, *SmartMoney* magazine's small business site. She has reported on a variety of issues facing small business owners, including cash flow management, health care and retirement planning, and the challenge of work/life balance.

Before joining *SmartMoney*, DeBaise spent seven years at Dow Jones Newswires as a personal finance columnist and also lead court reporter, covering the wave of corporate scandals that broke in 2002. Her stories have often appeared in *The Wall Street Journal*, *Chicago Tribune* and other news outlets. She has been interviewed on CNBC, MSNBC and Fox Business News.

DeBaise is a 2005 winner of the Newswomen's Club of New York's Front Page award for specialized writing. She has a master's degree from Northwestern University's Medill School of Journalism and a bachelor of arts in English from St. Lawrence University.

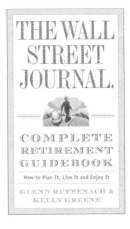

The Wall Street Journal
SPECIAL OFFER

The One Investment You Can Count On.

2 WEEKS FREE!

YES! Send me 2 free weeks of The Wall Street Journal and also enter my subscription for an additional 26 weeks at the money-saving rate of only $59.00 – just 39¢ a day! I receive 28 weeks in all and SAVE 69% off the regular rate.

Name

Address

City

State   Zip

2PFEN

CALL NOW FOR FASTER SERVICE!
1-800-620-5798

THE WALL STREET JOURNAL.

The Guide in your hands is a great way to start building wealth.

The best way to <u>keep your assets growing</u> is to read THE WALL STREET JOURNAL!

Weekend Journal: Music Stars Tell All About Their Summer Tours

THE WALL STREET JOURNAL.

Fed to Keep Lid on Bond Buys
Big Boost in Purchases Is Unlikely; Divisions Emerge Over Handling Risk of Inflation

Send in the card below and receive

2 WEEKS FREE!